READYMADE
CVs

A Source Book for Job Hunters

READYMADE
CVs

A Source Book for Job Hunters

LYNN WILLIAMS

KOGAN
PAGE

YOURS TO HAVE AND TO HOLD

BUT NOT TO COPY

First published in 1996
Reprinted 1997, 1998 (twice), 1999

Kogan Page Limited
120 Pentonville Road
London N1 9JN

British Library Cataloguing in Publication Data

A CIP record for this book is available from the British Library.

ISBN 0 7494 1947 4

Typeset by JS Typesetting, Wellingborough, Northants.
Printed in England by Clays Ltd, St Ives plc

Contents

How to use this book

Even just a few years ago, unless you were either very ambitious or very unlucky, you could expect to go to work in an organisation straight from school or college and stay there, gradually moving up the promotion ladder until you retired.

Today, career advancement is more uncertain. Most people will change jobs several times during their working lives, some will even change careers. Increasingly, a good CV is an essential tool in the survival kit of every employee.

What is a good CV though? The short answer is: one that gets you an interview for the job you want.

Imagine you're the employer for a moment. You have 150 CVs on your desk and from them you have to choose just a handful to interview further. What are you looking for? How do you decide? My bet is that you would pick people who look like they know how to do the job. People, that is, who:

- have the skills the job requires
- have experience relevant to the job
- have successfully handled similar challenges in the past

As an employer with 150 career histories to read, you would be grateful, too, to the people who made those facts easy to find on their CV.

This book is about making those facts easy to find, and how to highlight them to your best advantage. The first four chapters look in detail at what is in a CV – how to select what goes in and what stays out, layout and presentation, and how to make a good first impression.

Few people, however, have absolutely straightforward careers, and some CVs are trickier to write than others. So the next section – Chapters 4 to 8 – looks at some of the problems that people encounter, and how to handle them. It shows how, by highlighting key parts of your CV, you can emphasise your strengths rather than stressing your weaknesses. It also looks at CVs for specific 'tricky' situations – getting your first job, returning to work after a career break, continuing in work as a mature employee or after retirement.

The remaining chapters give further examples of CVs. These are written especially for specific categories of jobs – creative positions, sales vacancies, managerial posts, and so on.

Different types of job often emphasise different features when it comes to what makes a person right for that position. Some jobs rely heavily on personal qualities, some demand specific academic qualifications, while others require evidence of achievement in that particular field. These chapters show how, by highlighting and strengthening the relevant parts of your CV, you can emphasise these key points and put them across to a prospective employer effectively.

If you want to, you can follow the layout of the CV examples in this book to compile your own CV. Each, when typed or printed onto A4 paper, runs to two pages – the recommended length for a CV. Each example puts the key facts and the high priority information that tells an employer you know how to do the job on the front page, with back-up and lower-priority details on the second page.

Whether you're looking for your first job, aiming for promotion, or applying for the job of your dreams, you can put together a CV that shows your future employer your skills and experience clearly and concisely – these examples show you how.

1

The Basic CV

A CV, sometimes called a Curriculum Vitae or a résumé, is a summary of your career history, and the skills and experience you have gained during the course of it.

A good CV should:

- Attract attention
- Create a good impression
- Present your relevant skills and qualities clearly and concisely.

THE AIM OF A CV

The purpose of a CV is to show a prospective employer that you have the necessary qualities and qualifications to do the job you're applying for. Its aim is to get you an interview with that employer, so it needs to demonstrate clearly that you have:

- The specific skills needed for the job
- The right sort of experience for the job
- The personal qualities for this position
- An understanding of the specific requirements of the job.

Keep it simple

The easier a CV is to read the better. An advertised job vacancy will often attract hundreds of replies, and even the most conscientious employers have very little time to digest every CV that crosses their desk. The best way to make sure that yours gets read is to:

- **Keep it short.** No more than two A4 pages.
- **Keep it clear.** Make it easy to read. A CV should always be typewritten, and well laid out with wide margins, clear section headings, and the information organised in a logical, easy to follow way.
- **Keep it relevant.** The employer usually has two main questions in mind when looking at an employee or potential employee:
  — Is this person able to do the job?
  — Will this person fit in with the rest of us?

Create an impression

As well as keeping your CV short, clear and relevant, make it look business-like and professional too.

Use:

- plain white or cream A4 size paper
- good quality paper – 100 gsm weight
- a good, clear typeface
- plain black ink.

Avoid:

- gimmicks
- sending photocopies (unless they are very good quality)
- spelling and grammatical mistakes
- alterations and amendments – always print off a fresh, correct copy.

The following pages give a 'blueprint', showing what goes where, followed by a completed CV.

(**Your Name** in large, bold type)
(Your full address)

_____
_____
_____

(Postcode)

(Telephone number, including area code)

Personal Profile

(A brief, business-like description of yourself)

(Personal qualities)

(Experience)

(Skills and personal strengths)

Key Skills

- (The main skills you have developed)
- (Particularly those appropriate to the job you are applying for)
- _____
- _____
- _____

Career History

(**Name of Company**, usually starting with the most recent)

(Dates you worked there)

(Job title)

(Brief description of what you did)

(Brief description of what you achieved in this position)

- _____
- _____
- _____

(**Name of Company**)

(Dates you worked there)

(Job title)

(Brief description of what you did)

(Brief description of what you achieved in this position)

- _____
- _____
- _____

(**Name of Company**)

(Dates you worked there)

(Job title)

■ _____

(Brief description of what you did. Jobs you did some years ago require less detail than your more recent ones) _____

_____

_____

Education and Training

(Starting with the highest, most recent OR most relevant qualification)

(Name of school, college, or university) _____

(Dates you attended) _____

(The qualification you achieved) _____

(You could include brief details of what was covered in the course, especially if recently qualified) _____

- _____
- _____
- _____
- _____

(Name of school, college, or university) _____

(Dates you attended) _____

(The qualification you achieved) _____

(Name of school, college, or university) _____

(Dates you attended) _____

(The qualification you achieved) _____

(Don't go back further than your senior or secondary school)

(Professional Training)

(Details of any professional training undertaken at work)

- (Qualification or skill achieved) _____
- _____
- _____
- _____
- _____

Personal Details

(Date of birth) _____

(Driving licence) _____

(Married or single – only if relevant) _____

(Nationality – only if relevant) _____

(Interests and activities. Brief details) _____

_____

_____

(References – usually 'available on request') _____

Robert Dalesman
2 Woodland Drive
Sandacre
West Lea
Norfolk
NR4 5TE

Tel. 0100 0000000

Personal Profile

A self-motivated, ambitious and responsible company representative with experience of both sales and distribution, and the proven ability to consistently meet and surpass sales targets, now keen to move ahead in a challenging sales position. A good communicator at all levels who enjoys meeting challenges and seeing them through, while remaining good humoured under pressure. An experienced organiser and problem-solver, able to consider all options with an open mind before making a decision.

Key Skills

- Developing customer relationships from cold call to repeat order
- Recognising sales opportunities
- Identifying customer needs
- Organising daily and weekly schedules
- Managing customer credit control and discount negotiation
- Currently working towards Certificate in Sales and Marketing

Career History

Penbury Foods Ltd
1994 to present
Van Sales Representative
Delivered orders to current customers and developed new and existing accounts, including introduction of new lines and products.
   Turned a subsidised delivery route into a profit making sales territory:

- Reorganised two sales routes into one, thereby reducing costs
- Increased turnover by 55% in first six months
- Increased overall turnover by £2,500 per week

Dann Farms Ltd
1992 to 1994
Customer Deliveries Organizer
Organised weekly schedule of perishable product deliveries to supermarket outlets nationally. Supervised four-man delivery team, and liaised with Transport and Administration Department to coordinate delivery schedules.

Lockings Distribution
1987 to 1992
Van Driver
Part of the Locking Distribution Fleet. Delivered food products to supermarket chains, in accordance with a strict timetable. Maintained daily record logs. Responsible for maintaining vehicle to company standards. Promoted within company from previous position as general loader and driver.

Education and Training

Somerston College
1985 to 1987
City and Guilds Warehousing and Distribution

Lea Park School
1980 to 1985
Total of five GCSE 'O' levels gained, including Maths and English

Professional Training

Eastern Institute of Marketing
From September 1995

Certificate in Sales and Marketing
Two-year open learning course covering all aspects of professional sales including:
- Principles of selling
  - pricing and profit
  - negotiation
  - sales promotions
  - sales opportunities
  - advanced selling techniques
  - managing client accounts
  - developing client business
- Managing sales territories
- Finance for sales and marketing
- Law for sales and marketing
- Forecasting and analysis

Personal Details

Date of birth:	10 April 1969
Driving licence:	Full, clean UK
Interests:	A keen interest in sport and keeping fit, and play regularly for a local Sunday football team.
References:	Available on request

INCLUDE:

✓ **Your skills and experience, knowledge and capabilities.** Your relevant experience and competence are the most important things to put in your CV. Match them as closely as possible to those required by the job.

✓ **Skills and qualifications that feature in the job advertisement.** If you are answering an advertised vacancy, or if you have a comprehensive job description, make use of it. This is covered more fully in Chapter 4, Advertisements Into CVs.

✓ **Your achievements.** A CV is not the place for false modesty: achievements need to be spelled out clearly. Employers rarely have time to search out information, and should be able to see at a glance exactly what you can offer them.

✓ **Put the most important information on the first page.** If your CV runs to two pages, make sure the first page is the most interesting and highlights your key points.

LEAVE OUT:

✗ **Fussy, unnatural language.** Stick to plain language and clear, unambiguous statements.

✗ **Anything that sounds desperate.** It says, in effect, 'I'll do anything'.

✗ **Unnecessary personal details.** The less irrelevant information there is on the page the more clearly your achievements stand out. Unless you feel they are relevant, you can quite safely leave out the following:

Marital status	Religious affiliation
Maiden name	Political affiliation
Number of children	Age (in addition to date of birth)
Ages of children	Previous salary
Nationality	Reason for leaving last job
Gender	Photographs
Partner's occupation	

✗ **Negative information.** While it's unwise to lie in your CV, you don't have to include information that will diminish your chance of an interview – as long as it doesn't affect your ability to do the job. Always put things in the most positive way that you can.

✗ **Out-of-date and irrelevant information.** Things that happened more than ten years ago are of very little interest unless they have a direct bearing on your present capabilities. What you are doing currently is much more relevant.

✗ **References.** If references are required, they will be taken up later. There is no need to put the names and addresses of referees on your CV.

SHOULD I PUT IT IN OR LEAVE IT OUT?

There are two basic questions to ask yourself when considering whether or not to put an item of information into your CV:

- Will it encourage them to interview me?
- Will it discourage them from interviewing me?

If the answer to the first question is an emphatic yes, put it in. If, however, you feel less certain, think carefully about including it. Could the space be used more effectively to expand on something more important?

If you answer yes to the second question, leave it out.

CHECKLIST

- **Your finished CV should be:**
  — easy to read
  — easy to understand
  — attractive
  — present your skills, strengths, and achievements clearly
  — encourage the reader to want to interview you.
- **The layout of your CV**, the way it is actually arranged on the page, is important. Include:
  — wide margins
  — clear spacing
  — discreetly used capital letters, italics, and underlining to emphasise information
  — short, clearly headed, easy to read sections.

When you have written your CV, check the following points:

☐ Is the layout clear?
☐ Do the relevant points stand out?
☐ Is the language clear and understandable?

☐   Are your skills and achievements emphasised?
☐   Can the employer see the key points at a glance, or does the information have to be searched for and guessed at?
☐   Is it free of irrelevant details?
☐   Is it free of qualifying words such as fairly, usually and hopefully?
☐   Does a positive picture of you emerge?
☐   Is it well presented, smart and professional looking?

FINALLY

When you send your CV, remember the following:

- Always send your CV to a named individual within the company, not just to The Personnel Department. If you don't know the name of the person to send it to, ring up and find out.
- Include a covering letter written specifically to match the requirements of that job.
- The letter should be as well presented as your CV and typed on good quality, white or cream, A4 paper.
- Send your CV and covering letter unfolded in a white or cream A4 size envelope.
- If there is a closing date, make sure your application is sent off in good time. Applications received after the deadline are rarely, if ever, considered.

2

CVs Section by Section

Information is easier to understand when it's sorted into short, clearly labelled portions. As you may have already noticed, each CV in this book is divided into clear, easy to read sections:

Personal Profile
Key Skills
Career History
Education and Training
Personal Details

This chapter looks at each section in more detail, with further examples.

SECTION 1 – THE PERSONAL PROFILE

There are three types of personal statement:

a) Personal Profile
b) Career Profile
c) Career Objective

Each is a brief statement summarising either who you are, what you've done, or what you hope to do. These statements help to focus the rest of your CV, making what you have to offer stand out more clearly.

a) Personal Profile

This short statement outlines your personal characteristics. It gives an idea of the sort of person you are, your qualities and attributes, which may not otherwise be apparent from your CV.

(A brief, business-like description of yourself)

(Personal qualities)

(Experience)

(Skills and personal strengths)

Examples

- A smart, intelligent, experienced retail professional with an extensive background in fashion and women's wear both in large department stores and small boutiques. Creative, adaptable, versatile and, above all, tactful and diplomatic, with an excellent sense of colour and design.
- A mature and experienced trainer with a proven track record in the design and implementation of training, complemented by a background in counselling. A clear and concise communicator with the ability to motivate and encourage, along with a good ear for the underlying problems that can hinder efficient learning.
- An open-minded, outgoing and resourceful Project Leader with a sound background and optimistic outlook. Possessing a good sense of humour and the ability to develop and motivate others, coupled with the ability to communicate comfortably at all levels, thereby ensuring good teamwork and an energetic and productive working environment.
- An experienced creative all-rounder with enthusiasm and the proven ability to understand client needs and deliver satisfying solutions within a specified budget. A wide range of traditional skills complement the ability to use modern technology skilfully and appropriately. Highly developed communication skills fine-tuned by the need to deal effectively with people at all levels.
- A professional sales manager with an unusual breadth of experience in the international market. Dependable and energetic, with the ability to motivate and direct a workforce to meet targets and objectives, and with the persistence to achieve the highest standards in every undertaking.
- An innovative and intelligent electronics engineer, having designed and installed a range of systems for a variety of clients. Adept at working effectively within a multi-disciplined team at senior level, with many years' experience of understanding and evaluating problems in the field.
- Bilingual postgraduate – hardworking, self-motivated and responsible, with an articulate and outgoing personality. Enjoys meeting new challenges and seeing them through to completion, while remaining confident and good-humoured under pressure. An individual who

adapts well to new situations and has consistently worked effectively as a team member.

- A versatile and experienced administrator, proficient with both computerised and clerical systems. Quick to learn and skilled at working with people, analysing their problems and initiating an appropriate course of action. Capable of evaluating conflicting opinions and communicating the relevant information to the people who need to take action.
- A well-organised, reliable administrative assistant and secretary with extensive knowledge of good office practice, and a wealth of experience gained in both large and small companies. Hardworking and trustworthy, with the ability to remain good-humoured and unflappable under pressure.

The following things can be included when compiling a personal profile. See Chapter 3, Words and Phrases for further ideas and suggestions.

Personal qualities

- Self-motivated
- Creative
- Innovative
- Organized
- Adaptable
  etc.

Experience

- Ten years in sales management
- Wide experience of . . .
- A good working knowledge of . . .
- An excellent track record in . . .
- An extensive background in . . .
  etc.

Skills

- Management skills
- Communication skills
- Problem-solving skills
- Design skills
- Administrative skills
  etc.

Personal Strengths

- Works well under pressure
- An eye for detail
- Good sense of humour
- An effective, disciplined worker . . .
  etc.

b) Career Profile

Rather than concentrating on your personal characteristics, you may want to focus attention on your career highlights. A career profile outlines the key features of your work experience to date. It gives an idea of your background and capabilities, making it easier to pick out details from your CV.

Examples

- A highly trained sales professional with a thorough background in sales management, and specific experience in business-to-business negotiations. A successful, profit-driven individual with a proven track record in business systems, office supplies and business machines.
- A professional caterer with considerable experience in all aspects of catering and specific expertise in catering management for large-scale operations.
- A highly experienced, professional confectioner with a considerable background on all aspects of catering and retail disciplines through having started and developed a number of businesses in the field. A businessman with a thorough understanding of bookkeeping, marketing, stock control and staff management.
- A personal assistant and secretary with a background in several blue-chip companies and a thorough understanding of the computerised office, including word-processing and desktop publishing, electronic mail systems, spreadsheets and databases.
- A skilled translator fluent in Business Spanish having worked for the AngloBusiness Centre in Madrid, and for Compeco (Brazil) in England, with complementary office and computer skills. A Spanish-speaking graduate with excellent language skills developed through experience of teaching English as a Foreign Language in Spain, Portugal and Venezuela.
- A qualified counsellor with wide experience of advice work both with individuals and groups, and specific expertise in working with young people overcoming a variety of problems including drug and alcohol-related conditions.
- A qualified trainer for PC spreadsheets, data management and graphics presentation software, supported by expertise in information management and data analysis acquired in a range of business and financial environments.

Include the following in your career statement where appropriate:

What you are

- A professional manager
- A skilled administrator
- A qualified animal handler
- A trained conservator
- An experienced driver
  etc.

Your general experience

- with a technical background
- with wide experience of . . .
- with a strong background in . . .
- with a solid foundation in . . .
- with a successful career in . . .
- with a comprehensive knowledge of . . .
  etc.

Your specific skill areas

- with specific experience in . . .
- including a detailed knowledge of . . .
- with proven administrative and organisational skills
- with a strongly developed interest in . . .
- with a detailed understanding of . . .
  etc.

Significant accomplishments or achievements

- with a proven ability in . . .
- with an excellent track record in . . .
- having an excellent record of achievement in . . .
- having a highly developed . . .
  etc.

c) Career Objective

A career objective states the sort of position you are aiming for. It can be used on its own or combined with either of the types of statement above.

If you're making a speculative approach to a company, it can be useful for them to have a clear idea of what you're looking for.

If you're sending a CV in reply to an advertised vacancy, make sure that the job title and description in your career objective fit the ones in the advertisement.

Examples

- A competent, highly motivated project leader seeking a senior management position where enthusiasm, skill and experience can be put to good use in an environment where research produces solid end-results.
- Career objective – an administrative position where first rate word-processing and excellent interpersonal skills would be of value.
- A dynamic, people-oriented professional, interested in all types of communication, wishing to focus on a career in public relations where specific skills and experience can be put to effective use.
- A computer professional looking for a position in IT training using well-developed skills to help those people making the transition from 'streetfighter' to spreadsheets.
- A **chartered engineer** with ten years' experience in management, looking for a senior position where knowledge and skill will make a significant contribution towards corporate goals.
- An engineering graduate with a keen interest in computers seeking a career in computing, especially in a scientific or industrial field, where a background in problem solving would be an advantage.
- A versatile, quick thinking personal assistant looking for the opportunity to make use of an arts education in the field of publishing.
- A **systems analyst** with a background in business systems, interested in a position where the application of information technology can be used to improve company efficiency.

When compiling your career objective, include the following points:

- Say what you do – offer a job title or job description.
- Include some of your key strengths.
- Say where you're coming from – something about your background or experience.
- Say what you're aiming for – how you would like to use your skills and experience.

SECTION 2 – YOUR KEY SKILLS

Including a section highlighting your key skills can save anyone reading your CV a lot of time and effort.

The key skills section can be used to summarise and emphasise your:

- key skills and abilities or capabilities
- key qualifications
- key achievements.

-
- (The main skills you have developed)
- (Particularly those appropriate to the job you are applying for)
-
-
-

Key Skills

Example 1

- Management and supervision of staff
- An extensive knowledge of purchasing control
- The ability to operate an effective pricing policy
- An understanding of hygiene requirements at all point of contact
- A keen sense of the importance of margins and profits

Example 2

- Keyboard skills – 40 wpm
- Operation of
  — fax machine
  — photocopiers – Canon and Rank Xerox
  — franking machine
- Prepare and write routine correspondence
- Organise and carry out routine administrative work
  — maintaining records
  — dealing with incoming telephone calls
  — dealing with incoming mail

Example 3

- Carrying out routine security procedures
- Monitoring security equipment including alarms and surveillance cameras
- Checking and verifying all incoming personnel including deliveries
- Carrying out routine checking and maintenance of safety equipment

Key Qualifications

Example 1

- RSA III Typewriting – current speed 70 wpm
- RSA II Audio-typing – current speed 70 wpm
- RSA II Shorthand – current speed 120 wpm

- RSA Certificate in Computer Literacy and Information Technology:
  - Wordperfect 6.1
  - Word for Windows
  - Excel
  - dBase-3
  - Lotus

Example 2

- BSc Mechanical Engineering
- Practical experience of programming:
  - CNC machinery
  - CMM
  - Robots
- Use of CAD/CAM systems
- Computer programming languages:
  - 'C'
  - FORTRAN
  - COBOL

Key Achievements

Example 1

- Developing key ranges, many of which reached top ten leading brand status, including:
  - freeze dried pasta sauces
  - savoury snack rice
  - fresh chill soups
- Improving processing methods in natural set department, reducing spoilage and improving profit margins
- Reducing wastage in thick-set yoghurt department with similar effect
- Consistently bringing processing trials in to time and on budget

Example 2

- Initiating design services group specialising in high quality visual aids and display material, employing a team of eight designers and technicians
- Building up 'blue chip' client list, including ICL, Hewlett Packard, SmithKline Beecham, Manpower Services Commission, British Home Stores, Rolls Royce Aerospace
- Producing full marketing packages for London Manchester Insurance Group, ICI, South West Water, among others

- Liaising with Harpen Exhibition Group to produce Eurotech '94 in Brussels

Example 3

- Successfully managing, training and motivating 20 staff in three branches, thereby exceeding targets for insurance, savings, and mortgage lending sales
- Organising and opening two new suburban branch offices, and exceeding forecast transaction levels by 25% in the first year of operation
- Organising full relocation of group departments to new premises within strict deadlines
- Devising and delivering Lotus 1-2-3 training to Sales Support staff, enabling them to use data analysis tools; and to Secretarial staff, enabling them to produce presentations, graphs and organisation charts, and to maximise efficient system usage
- Designing and providing user-friendly computer spreadsheet for Commercial Lending Sales Team, enabling them to project lending terms and reduction of capital balances for given varying repayment possibilities

SECTION 3 – YOUR CAREER HISTORY

Your career history tells a prospective employer what you have done and where and when you have done it.

For each entry in your career history section, include:

- The name of the company
- The dates you worked there
- Your job title or position
- The main responsibilities of that position
- Your key achievements during your time there

(**Name of Company**, usually starting with the most recent)

(Dates you worked there)

(Job title)

(Brief description of what you did)

(Brief description of what you achieved in this position)

-
-
-

26

Example 1
K&L Polton
1990 to 1995
Human Resources Manager
Trained, assessed and developed staff at all levels
- Responsible for 750 employees
- Devised and introduced new appraisal system for all departments, based on performance assessment and linked to performance-related pay structure
- Trained in-house assessors for new system
- Initiated use of interactive software for staff development in areas other than IT training
- Supervised a professional training team of 10

Example 2
Axon Business Machines
1990–1994
Sales Executive
Appointed to direct sales role. Responsible for meeting targets on sales of office equipment in business-to-business environment.
  Achievements include:
- Directed highly successful sales team to top company awards
- Increased profit margins by more than 10%
- Won Top Salesperson Award two years in succession
- Achieved more than 100% increase in technical support revenue budgets

Example 3
Safe As Houses
1989 to Present
Volunteer Counsellor
Counselled young people with a variety of problems centring on homelessness. Managed a heavy caseload, giving advice and information on housing and benefit entitlements where appropriate, and participated in supervision and support meetings. Attended residential course on Means Tested Benefits by the Welfare Rights Unit.

Example 4
Peel Supplies Ltd.
1991 – Present
Warehouse and Distribution Supervisor
- Supervised 25 full-time staff, rising to 35 at peak periods
- Instructed and monitored incoming trainees

- Verified and processed orders
- Introduced and established incentive scheme which reduced petty pilfering by 75%
- Promoted from Warehouse Assistant to Warehouse and Distribution Supervisor in 1993

Example 5
Eight 'til Late Shop, Bartonbury
1992 to 1994
Cashier and Kiosk Assistant
General care of stock:
- Checked deliveries
- Replenished shelves
- Ordered stock using computerised system

Cash handling:
- Cashier duties, including balancing tills
- Handled upwards of £5,000 per day

Customer care:
- Served and assisted customers
- Handled enquiries and complaints
- Responsible for alcohol and cigarette legislation

Example 6
The Woodland School Project, Bannham
Summer 1993 and 1995
Drama Instructor
Worked as part of a team to plan and implement out-of-school drama project for 70 mixed ability students aged 8 to 11. Taught performance techniques, monitored students' progress, maintained records. Coached and motivated to production standard, set goals to encourage performance levels.

SECTION 4 – YOUR EDUCATION AND TRAINING

If you have just left school, college or university, this section will probably take a higher priority and include more detailed information. If, however, you have more than two years' experience of working, your career details will be of more interest to a prospective employer.

Education and training can include:

- Academic achievements, diplomas and degrees, etc.
- Professional qualifications
- Technical qualifications
- Vocational training where relevant
- Relevant company training programmes
- Computer skills and training
- Language skills
- Professional membership of relevant associations

(Starting with the highest, most recent OR most relevant qualification)
(Name of school, college, or university)

(Dates you attended)

(The qualification you achieved)

(You could include brief details of what was covered in the course, especially if recently qualified)

-
-
-
-

(Professional Training)

(Details of any professional training undertaken at work)

- (Qualification or skill achieved)
-
-
-

Example 1
West Midlands University
1992–1995
BSc Computer Science

- Robotics – concepts, VAL, 3-D modelling of component assembly, matrices
- Graphics – 2-D and 3-D, projection, transformation matrices
- Communications – network theory, protocols, hardware
- Database Theory – structure storage, design
- Formal Logic – trinary, fuzzy, temporal
- Artificial Intelligence – Popll, expert systems, Prolog, theory of neural nets

Example 2

1994 University of the South
   Postgraduate Diploma in European Business Administration

1992 Institute of Linguists
   Institute of Linguists Intermediate Diploma in German

1992 UOS School of Business
   RSA Preparatory Certificate Teaching English as a Foreign Language

1990 London Polytechnic
   BA Hons English and German Literature 2:1

Example 2

1990–1992 Westbrook College of Further Education
   Certificate of Counselling Theory AEB/CAC
   Certificate of Counselling Practice AEB/CAC

1991–1994 Forest Community College
   Open Access vocational courses:
   - Post-Trauma Stress and Critical Incident Debriefing
   - Primary Health Care Counselling
   - Managing Short-Term Counselling Work within Primary Care
   - Women and Mental Health

Example 3
Professional Qualifications

1995	Diploma in Marketing	Institute of Marketing
1993	Certified Diploma in Accounting and Finance	Chartered Association of Accountants
1985	Diploma in Management Studies	Westland College
1983	BSc Hons Degree Economics	University of Dorset

Professional Training
Computer Skills
  - Computerised Accounting
  - Using Microsoft Excel
  - Excel for Windows
  - Databases with Paradox 4
  - Integrated Business Technology

Language Skills
- – Fluent conversational and business German
- – Competent spoken French

Member of the Institute of Marketing

Example 4
1987–1990 Collworth College of Technology
      BTEC HND Food Technology
      Access to Science Course

1982–1987 Albert Ellis High School
      3 GCE 'A' levels: Economics, French, English
      5 GCSE 'O' levels including Maths and English

SECTION 5 - YOUR PERSONAL DETAILS

The details often covered in this section include:

Personal details
- date of birth
- possession of a clean driving licence
- marital status – if absolutely relevant
- nationality – if relevant
- special details such as a registered disability.

Interests and activities
- brief details of anything that will add to or support the picture of yourself you are presenting.

References
- usually covered by 'available on request' unless you have something really spectacular to offer.

(Date of birth)
_____

(Driving licence)
_____

(Married or single – only if relevant)
_____

(Nationality – only if relevant)
_____

(Interests and activities. Brief details)

(References – usually 'available on request')

Example 1
Date of birth: 15 November 1965
Driver: Car owner, full, clean, UK licence
Interests: Team sports – netball, volleyball. Running.
                      Took part in London Marathon in 1993
References: Available on request

Example 2
Date of birth: 1 January 1975
Relocation: Prepared to relocate
Interests: Reading, singing and writing. I have frequently
                      sung in a professional capacity, and have
                      appeared as an extra for both the BBC and
                      HTV and am a member of Equity. Produced
                      several shows and plays for the local dramatic
                      society.
References: Available on request.

Example 3
Date of birth: 25 May 1957
Licence: Full, clean, UK driving licence
Health: Non-smoker
Interests: All aspects of conservation work including the
                      National Trust for Conservation, World Wide
                      Fund for Nature, and the RSPB. Chair of the
                      local conservation group, and have organised
                      and participated in several local projects.
References: Available on request.

3

Words and Phrases

Finding the right word is often one of the hardest parts of writing a CV. This chapter has examples of positive words and phrases for you to use, and which might also remind you of skills and qualities you may want to include. It contains:

- Positive characteristics
- Action words
- Positive descriptions
- Benefits and achievements
- Desirable qualities

POSITIVE CHARACTERISTICS

These words describe personal attributes that are often seen as positive and useful in the workplace. Choose the words that describe you best:

Able	Attractive	Decisive
Accurate		Dedicated
Adaptable	Bilingual	Dependable
Adroit	Bright	Diligent
Adventurous		Diplomatic
Alert	Calm	Dynamic
Ambitious	Capable	
Analytical	Competent	Educated
Appreciative	Confident	Effective
Articulate	Consistent	Efficient
Assertive	Cooperative	Energetic
Astute	Creative	Enthusiastic

Experienced
Expert

Fast
Firm
Fit
Flexible
Friendly

Gregarious

Hardworking
Healthy
Honest
Human
Humane

Imaginative
Independent
Informed
Ingenious
Innovative
Intelligent
Inventive

Knowledgeable

Literate
Loyal

Mature
Methodical
Motivated
Multilingual

Non-smoking

Objective
Open-minded
Organised
Outgoing
Outstanding

Patient
People-oriented
Perceptive
Persistent
Personable
Pioneering
Poised
Practical
Principled
Productive
Professional
Proficient
Punctual

Qualified
Quick
Quick-thinking

Rational
Ready
Realistic
Reliable
Resourceful
Responsible
Robust

Scrupulous
Self-assured
Self-confident
Self-motivated
Self-reliant
Sensitive
Serious
Shrewd
Skilled
Smart
Spirited
Stable
Strong
Successful
Supportive

Tactful
Talented
Tenacious
Thorough
Thoughtful
Trained
Trustworthy

Versatile
Vigorous

Well-educated
Well-groomed
Willing
Witty

Young
Youthful

ACTION WORDS

These are positive, active words that you can use to describe your responsibilities and achievements.

(All the words here are in the past tense – they all end in 'ed' – which is right for the Career History section of your CV. If you want to use them in the Key Skills section, change the 'ed to 'ing' to turn it into the present tense; for example:

Key Skills: Organising meetings and functions, purchasing stationery
Career History: Organised meetings and functions, purchased stationery)

Accelerated
Accessed
Achieved
Acquired
Acted
Administered
Advised
Analysed
Appointed
Appraised
Arranged
Assigned
Assisted
Attended

Booked
Broadened
Budgeted

Checked
Coached
Collaborated
Competed
Completed
Communicated
Compiled
Conceived
Conducted
Consulted
Contributed
Controlled
Coordinated
Correlated
Created

Delegated
Demonstrated
Designed
Determined
Developed

Devised
Diagnosed
Directed
Doubled

Edited
Effected
Eliminated
Enabled
Established
Evaluated
Executed
Exercised
Expanded
Expedited
Explored

Facilitated
Fostered
Formulated
Founded

Generated
Guided

Handled
Harmonised
Headed
Helped
Hired

Identified
Implemented
Improved
Increased
Initiated
Installed
Instituted
Instructed
Interacted

Invented
Investigated

Launched
Led
Liaised

Maintained
Managed
Marketed
Mentored
Monitored
Motivated

Negotiated

Opened
Operated
Organised
Oversaw

Participated
Performed
Pinpointed
Pioneered
Planned
Prepared
Presented
Processed
Produced
Programmed
Promoted
Proposed
Provided
Purchased

Recommended
Recruited
Recorded
Reduced

Reorganised	Scheduled	Tested
Reported	Secured	Trained
Represented	Selected	
Researched	Set up	Upgraded
Resolved	Shaped	Used
Restored	Sold	Utilised
Restructured	Solved	
Reviewed	Structured	Visualised
Revised	Supervised	
		Won
Saved	Taught	Wrote

POSITIVE DESCRIPTIONS

As well as using positive words for your characteristics and achievements, there are also a variety of ways to describe your strengths. Instead of saying 'I am good at . . .', you could say:

Skilled at . . .	Excelling at . . .
A skilful . . .	With the ability to . . .
Possessing a degree of ability in . . .	Competent in . . .
Very good at . . .	An experienced . . .
Extremely good at . . .	A deft . . .
Exceptional at . . .	A talent for . . .
Adept at . . .	Familiar with . . .
An expert in . . .	Qualified to . . .

For example:

- Skilled at facilitating the exchange of ideas
- A skilful communicator
- With a high degree of ability in computer programming
- Adept at promoting policy changes
- Very good at handling a variety of tasks efficiently
- Exceptional at motivating large or small groups
- Having a talent for budget projection
- Familiar with a wide range of software
- Qualified to assess retail training up to NVQ level 3

BENEFITS

Employers want to feel confident that the person they employ will take problems off their hands. They are looking for people who can do any of the following:

Increase	Decrease	Improve
Profits	Staff turnover	Competitive advantage
Product turnover	Risks	Appearance and/or marketability
Sales	Time taken	Organisation
Efficiency	Potential problems	Information flow
Market opportunities	Costs	Staff performance
	Waste	Teamwork and relationships

Make sure your CV includes any of the above benefits that you have achieved in your job.

DESIRABLE QUALITIES

The following characteristics are rated the most desirable by the majority of employers. Although many of them seem quite obvious, they are the sort of things that can easily be forgotten when thinking about your qualities and characteristics. Bear them in mind when compiling your CV and include them, where relevant and appropriate, in your Personal Profile or Career Profile.

Employers prefer someone who is:
Reliable
Punctual
Trustworthy
Friendly
Willing to learn
Enthusiastic
Accurate
Able to work as part of a team
Able to follow instruction accurately
Able to handle problems, and refer them on, appropriately
Able to work with customers or clients.

Employers look for someone who:
Has a positive attitude
Takes pride in their work
Has a suitable appearance
Has initiative.

Employers would rather not employ people who are:
Dishonest
Unreliable
Irresponsible
Arrogant
Bad at time-keeping and unpunctual
Unable to follow instructions
Constant complainers
Lacking motivation
Lacking enthusiasm

. . . however highly skilled or qualified they may otherwise be.

PUTTING IT TOGETHER

Use the 'blueprint' CV on the next page as a guide to where you might find suitable words and phrases for each particular section.

Play around with the words in this chapter and the examples in Chapter 2 until you arrive at something that describes both you and the work you have done, accurately and positively.

If you are replying to an advertised vacancy, the job advertisement itself might contain some ideas. Read several ads for the sort of job you intend to apply for to give you a feel for the sort of descriptive words that are used in your particular field. You can include those that apply to you in your CV. See Chapter 4, Advertisements into CVs, for more on this topic.

_____

Personal Profile

(Look at **Positive Characteristics, Positive Descriptions,** and **Desirable Qualities**)

_____

_____

_____

Key Skills

(Look at **Positive Descriptions** and _____

- **Action Words**) _____
- _____
- _____
- _____

Career History

(Name of Company) _____

(Dates you worked there) _____

(Job title) _____

(Job responsibilities. Look at **Action Words**) _____

- (Achievements and responsibilities. Look at **Action Words,**
- and **Benefits**) _____
- _____
- _____

(Name of Company) _____

(Dates you worked there) _____

(Job title) _____

(Job responsibilities. Look at **Action Words**) _____

- (Achievements and responsibilities. Look at **Action Words,**
- and **Benefits**) _____
- _____
- _____

4

Advertisements into CVs

Many job advertisements tell you a lot about what to put in your CV. As well as the local and national newspapers, the best place to look for advertised vacancies is in the journals and magazines associated with your particular trade or profession.

When you find an ad for a job you particularly want, it's worth studying it carefully before responding, and drafting a fresh CV using the advertisement as a guideline. You need to:

- Analyse what they want
- Assess what you've got to offer
- Match the two as closely as possible on your CV.

The key requirements in the following job-advertisement have been used as pointers to writing a CV specifically for the position.

Office Administrator

Rapidly expanding business in city centre urgently requires experienced person to provide administrative and secretarial support. Must be competent in Word for Windows and dBase III. Will also be required to provide customer support both over the phone and in writing, so excellent telephone manner essential and background in customer service or telesales an advantage. Must be able to work on own initiative without supervision and have a flexible approach to working hours. Some bookkeeping experience and familiarity with spreadsheets would be an advantage, but training will be given to the right candidate.

THEY WANT:

- Administrative and secretarial experience
- Computer skills:
  - Word 6.0 for Windows
  - dBase III
- Confident telephone manner
- Ability to work on own initiative
- A flexible approach to working hours
- Experience of customer services and/or telesales
- Some bookkeeping experience
- Familiarity with spreadsheets.

The overall style and tone of the ad suggests they would also like someone:

- used to responsibility
- confident and helpful
- willing to learn
- energetic and business-like – the same style the advertisement is written in
- dependable, and able to work alone
- able to cope with pressure – the company is expanding rapidly
- able to deal with routine without getting bored – a large part of the job is secretarial and administrative.

USE THE ADVERTISEMENT TO COMPILE YOUR CV

Once you have assessed what the advertiser is asking for, you can make good use of the information in the advertisement by:

- using words and phrases that appear in the advertisement
- selecting – from a much wider range of possibilities – the skills and experience specifically requested in the ad.
- putting the points relating to the ad in *first* – other points can be added after. The more information you add, however, the less clearly these key points will stand out
- including *all* your relevant qualifications and experience.

On the next two pages an applicant for the Office Administrator's job has started to compile her CV using the job advertisement as a guide to the important points that must be included. Note that the CV:

- includes a Career Profile written especially for this job
- selects the Key Skills specifically mentioned in the advertisement
- highlights the three previous jobs that correspond most closely to the job requirements
- emphasises relevant training and experience even where, as with bookkeeping experience, this has been gained outside of paid work.

Anyone reading this CV can tell, almost at a glance, that the applicant has nearly all the qualities they are looking for, making it very easy to pick this person for an interview.

_____

_____

_____

_____

Career Profile

(Include key words from the advertisement)

Experienced office administrator   secretary

competent   flexible   responsible   confident

background in customer relations

looking for opportunity and challenge with an expanding/developing company

Key Skills

(Include key skills and/or qualifications requested in the advertisement)

- Five years experience of administrative and secretarial work
- Experience in Customer Services
- Computer skills include:
  — Word 6.0 for Windows
  — dBase III
  — Word Perfect 5.1
- Keyboard 60 wpm plus proficient shorthand and audio typing
- Confident telephone manner
- Experience of working on own initiative
- Bookkeeping experience and familiarity with spreadsheets

Career History

(Relate responsibilities and experience to those asked for in the advertisement)

_____

Administrator
Provided administrative support for personnel and training department
- Maintained personnel and payroll database
- Organised and co-ordinated all appointments and bookings
- Liaised with personnel in all offices re departmental issues
- Dealt with enquiries and handled all general administrative matters

_____

Secretary
Provided secretarial service to Sales team
- Word-processed reports, letters and general correspondence
- Serviced incoming mail
- Prioritised own workload.

_____

Customer Relations Adviser
Responsible for providing telephone service for clients
- Dealt with customer enquiries in a competent and friendly manner
- Provided accurate product information
- Assessed queries and complaints and initiated appropriate follow-up action

_____

Clerk

_____

Clerical Assistant

Education and Training

- NVQ level 2 Office Administration
- CLAIT certificate including:
  — Lotus 123 spreadsheet
  — Word for Windows
  — Excel for Windows

Personal Details

Interests: Treasurer of local Civic Society which includes:
                   Bookkeeping
                   Maintenance of accounts using Lotus spreadsheet
                   Preparing books for auditing

5

Problems, Problems

Overcoming problems is often a matter of emphasising some sections of your CV and playing down others. This chapter looks at how this applies to 21 of the most common problems in CV writing.

PROBLEM 1. 'MY CV WOULD FILL FOUR PAGES, AT LEAST'

The things you have done recently are more important to a prospective employer than things you did years ago. Highlight the skills which are most relevant to the job you are applying for. Detail your recent experience and summarise everything else.

Example
Career Profile *(Give a brief career summary)*
A skilled engineer with over 20 years' manufacturing experience in the engineering and furniture industries, including ten years at senior management level. Currently developing a competitively driven organisation demanding high standards of performance.

Key Skills *(Choose the most relevant ones)*
- Operations and manufacturing management
- Logistics management using current tools and techniques
- Staff management: development and management of change strategy
- Financial management control, budget preparation
- Project management

Career History *(Go into detail about your current job . . .)*
Pitman Ltd, Limpsfield
1987 to Present
Operations Manager
Responsible for factories and staff within Operations Group

- Reorganised profile business and set up Logistics Support Centre, reducing operating costs by £150K
- Coordinated and managed activities in five factories and Logistics Support Centre, ensured effective running of operations supplying products to customers
- Formulated and implemented change programme in three factories to bring them level with rest of group
- Improved industrial relations, restoring management leadership with help of Partnership Agreement
- Increased financial performance of group by £300K overall
- Promoted to present position from Factory Manager 1992

Vollens Engineering, Stoke
1983 to 1987
Industrial Engineer *(. . . briefly summarise earlier, less relevant ones)*
Industrial engineering services at factory and divisional level. Provided production engineering service with particular emphasis on product costing, value engineering, pre-production engineering and methods improvement.

PROBLEM 2. 'I'VE JUST LEFT SCHOOL/COLLEGE/ UNIVERSITY. WHAT DO I PUT IN MY CV?'

This topic is covered fully in Chapter 6, Starting Out.

PROBLEM 3. 'MY WORK HISTORY ISN'T STRAIGHTFORWARD'

Summarise the main themes of your career history in a Profile at the top of your CV. Organise the skills and experience you have acquired into groupings under appropriate headings, so that the full range of your skills is covered. If you have a wide range of skills, select those that are the most appropriate to the job you are applying for.

Example
Personal Profile *(Emphasise any common threads or themes in your career)*
Energetic, adaptable and versatile, with a sound background and useful experience in both sales and business management. A quick learner possessing a good sense of humour and a flexible approach, coupled with the ability to communicate comfortably at all levels, thereby ensuring good teamwork and a productive working environment.

Career Objective *(Tell them where you're heading now)*
A sales position where a business background and excellent interpersonal skills would be of value.

Key Skills
Sales
- Maintaining and servicing existing accounts while developing new territory
- Liaising with distribution department to ensure efficient service to customers
- Developing new sales drive offering extended range of products to existing customers
- Producing quarterly analysis of sales by product and customer for head office records

Business Management
- Managing businesses, including a busy town centre café, requiring a range of skills, including:
  — Purchasing stock
  — Establishing pricing structures
  — Marketing and promotion
  — Bookkeeping
  — Managing staff

Career History *(If your work history is confusing, summarise it briefly)*

1993–Present	Sales Representative	Bullseye Windows, Deanleigh
1991–1993	Manager	Corner's Cafe, Penbury
1987–1991	Manager	Dilly's Gifts, Fosbury
1985–1987	Sales Assistant	Dean Catering, Deansgate
1985–1985	Telesales Representative	Homer Ltd, Penbury
1981 - 1985	Cellerman and foodstoreman	Foss Hotel, Fosbury

PROBLEM 4. 'I'M DOING MORE THAN ONE JOB'

This situation is becoming more and more common as people adapt to different career structures. You may be doing two part-time jobs instead of one full-time one, or you may be self-employed and also doing a part-time job, or a 'portfolio' worker with several strings to your bow, or a full-timer working on freelance contracts in your own time.

As shown in Problem 3 above, summarise the main theme of your career in a Profile, and organise your range of skills and experience under separate headings. When you come to your Career History, group your jobs together under the relevant date.

Example
Career History
1990 to Present
Video Maker
Community Production Facility
— Planned, produced and directed seven 30–60 minute videos for The Parenting Initiative
— Decided with featured experts content and presentation of video
— Planned lighting, camera angles, camera shots
— Designed, produced and directed two independent video shorts

Radio Producer and Presenter
Valley Radio
— Researched, planned and presented weekly community arts slot on local radio
— Delivered reports
— Selected, approached and interviewed guests

Video Trainer/Facilitator
Kids TV
Community Youth Group
— Assisted youth group making youth and community videos
— Trained them in use of video equipment and basics of production and editing
— Coordinated sound, content and storyline

PROBLEM 5. 'I'VE HAD A LOT OF JOBS'

Condense your employment record, focusing attention on the skills you have achieved through your experience, and only giving details of your most recent and most relevant positions. Jobs held more than ten or 15 years ago can often be lumped together as 'various'.

Example
Employment Record

1990–Present	Logistica Ltd., Gwent **Production Manager**
1983–1990	Owen Pearson, Gwent **Factory Manager** **Industrial Engineer (promoted 1987)**
1977–1983	Various **Engineering and supervisory**

PROBLEM 6. 'I'M CHANGING CAREERS'

Use a Career Objective at the head of your CV to make your new direction clear. Pick out your skills, qualities and achievements that are most appropriate to your new career and emphasise these.

Example
Career Objective

To use and expand my existing skills in a challenging and worthwhile situation which is counselling related, where there is opportunity for further personal development and learning.

Key Qualifications
- Certificate of Counselling Practice (AEB)
- Certificate of Counselling Theory (AEB)

Career History
Volunteer Counsellor

Safe As Houses
1989 to Present
Counselled young people with a variety of problems centring on home-lessness. Managed a heavy caseload, giving advice and information on housing and benefit entitlements where appropriate, and participated

in supervision and support meetings. Attended residential course on Means Tested Benefits by the Welfare Rights Unit.

Sales Receptionist
SAR TV & Video rentals
1990 to 1993
Demonstrated, sold and arranged rentals of TVs and videos, handled cash and security, stock control, telephone enquiries and customer accounts.

PROBLEM 7. 'MY RELEVANT EXPERIENCE IS IN VOLUNTARY/UNPAID WORK'

Voluntary positions are acceptable as part of your career history. The skills and experience you have gained from the job are as important as those gained from paid employment. Include them.

PROBLEM 8. 'I HAVEN'T GOT MUCH EXPERIENCE FOR THE JOB I WANT TO DO'

Make the most of what you can offer. Look at your qualifications, training, current experience – including both paid and unpaid work – and personal qualities. Make full use of Key Skills, Key Achievement or Key Experience sections, whichever seems appropriate, to highlight those that match the job you want. Don't leave potential employers to dig these important details out of your CV for themselves.

If lack of experience is a serious handicap, consider 'alternative' ways of getting it, such as volunteering, an unpaid work-experience placement, temporary or part-time work, short-term contracts, or even taking a step down the career ladder in order to work your way up to a new position.

PROBLEM 9. 'MOST OF THE JOBS I'VE DONE HAVE BEEN VERY MUCH THE SAME'

Concentrate on your key skills and achievements and simply summarise your actual career history.

Example
Career Profile
A smart, efficient sales consultant and confident in-store demonstrator, experienced in a number of sales environments including TV and video, white goods, and home furnishings.

Key Skills
- Customer care
- Cash handling and security
- Stock control, including operating computerised stock control system
- Financial administration, including credit agreements, customer accounts, credit/debit notes, and bank reconciliations
- Clerical administration, including sales reports and customer correspondence

Key Achievements
- Organised and managed Sandlands stand at this year's Home Electric Exhibition
- Used computerised stock control system to track and analyse stock movement between five branches
- Organised daily bank deposits of cash and credit card takings
- Member of team winning 'Contact '94' award

Employment Record

1992–Present	Sandlands Sales and Marketing **Sales Demonstrator**
1989–1992	TV Ten TV & Video Rentals **Sales Consultant**
1987–1989	Whittaker Furnishings **Sales Consultant**

PROBLEM 10. 'I KNOW I'M RIGHT FOR THE JOB, BUT HOW CAN I GET THAT ACROSS?'

Special jobs deserve special preparation. When you find a job that you know is just what you're looking for, take the time and trouble to prepare a CV specifically for that vacancy, using the skills and qualities listed in the job advertisement or job description. Carefully match your own qualifications and experience with the employer's needs.

Chapter 4, Advertisements Into CVs, has more information about doing this.

PROBLEM 11. 'I'M OVER-QUALIFIED FOR THE JOB I WANT'

Emphasise the relevant *practical* skills and experience that you have for the job. Focus attention on your Key Skills section, and choose the skills that fit the job you are applying for. 'Excess' qualifications can be discreetly mentioned in the education section. Highlight, instead, any relevant on-the-job training you have had.

PROBLEM 12. 'I DON'T HAVE MANY QUALIFICATIONS'

Concentrate on what you do have. Emphasise your practical skills and experience; these are often more valuable to an employer than theoretical knowledge anyway.

If your lack of qualifications is becoming a serious handicap to your progress, consider applying for further training. This can, increasingly, be undertaken in the workplace without the need to go back to full-time education for two or three years. You may also find that your existing experience can be counted towards a qualification.

Example
Key Skills
Customer Care
- Receive and seat customers
- Take orders from customers and liaise with the kitchen
- Handle customer enquiries and complaints efficiently

Service
- Provide both à la carte and table d'hôte style service
- Perform silver service and French style food service
- Set tables for meals of up to eight courses
- Serve wine and other beverages
- Clear tables systematically

Key Achievements
- Provided silver service at city centre four star hotel, serving up to 600 people daily at breakfast, lunch and dinner
- Performed waitress service and bar service at major functions
- Served all types and levels of customers efficiently, pleasantly and courteously

PROBLEM 13. 'I'M OVER 50'

Make sure your CV clearly states your experience and successful track record – these things tend to come only with maturity - and stringently edit your early career history.

This subject is covered more fully in Chapter 8, Keeping Going.

PROBLEM 14. 'I'M UNDER 25'

You may be lacking experience. Make full use of any experience you do have, and highlight any skills you may have from school or college, even if you haven't had the opportunity to use them in a work setting.

This subject is covered more fully in Chapter 6, Starting Out.

PROBLEM 15. 'I'M RETURNING TO WORK AFTER BRINGING UP CHILDREN'

Stress your capabilities, qualities and experience. Highlight any skills you have gained in voluntary positions in the home, school, or in the community, as well as any training or re-training you may be doing in preparation for your return to work.

This subject is covered more full in Chapter 7, Starting Again.

PROBLEM 16. 'I'M APPLYING FOR TWO DIFFERENT TYPES OF JOBS'

If you're applying for different types of job requiring different abilities and qualities, you will need to have two different CVs, each with a different emphasis.

The following two CVs have been prepared for the same person, the first concentrating on training experience and the second concentrating on sales experience:

Guy Owen

33 Holly Court
Prince's Road
Leeds, LS5 2AS

Telephone: 00000 0000000

Career Profile

A skilled and experienced trainer with over 12 years' experience in training and allied fields. Currently undertaking a wide range of consultative training initiatives in both the private and public sector. Also responsible for the effective coordination of professional services within the company.

Training Experience

- Successfully trained and licensed a sales force of 50 within three months
- Designed and implemented a new monitoring and assessment system
- Established management training for Branch Sales Managers
- Consistently achieved sales training targets
- Devised and wrote training manuals
- Awarded Technical Training Prize 1988 and 1989

Career Summary

1992–Present	Training Consultant	ICS Training
1989–1992	Area Sales Manager	Ellenbach Assurance
1985–1989	Head of Sales Training	Mutual Assurance Financiers
1980–1985	Sales Manager	Bradford-Bond Brokerage
1977–1980	Sales Associate	Crown Corporate Investments

Education and Training

1985	ASA Associates:	Certificate in Training
1975–1977	South Bradley College:	HNC Business Studies

Member of the Life Assurance Association

Personal

Date of birth: 17 November 1957

Full, clean UK driving licence

References available on request

Guy Owen
33 Holly Court
Prince's Road
Leeds
LS5 2AS

Telephone: 0000 0000000

Career Objective

A Senior Sales Executive with many years' experience looking for a position where an understanding of sales and marketing can be put to good use in achieving major business goals. Familiar with and enjoying the challenge of an innovative environment working to exacting deadlines and targets, and looking forward to new opportunities for leadership, having demonstrated clear capabilities for communication and presentation, and able to relate successfully to people at all levels.

Sales Experience

- Personal sales track record in direct selling with a client base exceeding 600 in five years
- Increased sales by 20 per cent over preceding year's totals
- Formulated major policy decisions on all stages of sales activities
- Responsible for new product launches
- Achieved competitive advantage through thorough knowledge of the market
- Successfully set up sales training programme

Career Summary

1992–Present	Training Consultant	ICS Training
1989–1992	Area Sales Manager	Ellenbach Assurance
1985–1989	Head of Sales Training	Mutual Assurance Financiers
1980–1985	Sales Manager	Bradford-Bond Brokerage
1977–1980	Sales Associate	Crown Corporate Investments

Education and Training

1975–1977	South Bradley College	HNC Business Studies
1985	ASA Associates	Certificate in Training

Member of the Life Assurance Association

Personal

Date of birth: 17 November 1957

Full, clean UK driving licence

References available on request

PROBLEM 17. 'I'VE BEEN UNEMPLOYED FOR OVER A YEAR'

As with many of the problems above, the answer is to draw attention to your positive points and give these the major share of your CV, and to cover only briefly those areas where you may be weaker.

Include the skills you have learned through voluntary work or further training during your period of unemployment. In the example below, the job as Finance Administrator was a full-time voluntary position, but attention isn't drawn to this fact.

Example
Key Skills
Management
- Managing and motivating five full-time and up to 20 part-time staff in three branches
- Maximising savings, mortgage sales, and introducing customer services including mortgage debt counselling
- Exceeding targets set for insurance, savings and mortgage lending sales
- Representing Mutual Assurance Group on committee of local Chamber of Commerce

Financial Administration
- Running purchase order system and budget control
- Preparing month-end accounts and monthly business reports
- Compiling Management Information Reports and preparing claims for Government Agencies
- Organising and administering payment of office and staff expenses

Information Technology
- Proficient in using both spreadsheet and word-processing applications:
- Supercalc 5.5
- Excel 5.0
- Access 2.0
- Wordperfect 5.1
- Word 6.0 for Windows

Career Summary

Currently	Information Technology NVQ level 3	Data Training
1993–1994	Finance Administrator	Cosmopolitan Trust
1989–1993	Group Branch Manager	Mutual Assurance Group
1980–1989	Travel Agency Manager	Bond Travel

PROBLEM 18. 'I HAVE TWO QUITE DIFFERENT AREAS OF EXPERIENCE'

This is similar to Problem 16. Consider preparing two quite different CVs, each highlighting one of your two main areas of experience.

PROBLEM 19. 'MY LAST JOB WAS ACTUALLY A BIT OF A STEP BACKWARDS (OR SIDEWAYS)'

With so many organisations changing their structure and, sometimes, even cutting out whole layers of management, this is true for many people these days.

Don't draw attention to it. Put your abilities and achievements in a separate, major, section and just summarise the rest of your employment details.

Example
Key Skills

- Providing a Help Desk for software and hardware queries
- Using VMS and RSX operating systems to recover lost data files
- Analysing system performance, identifying problems and establishing their probable origin before taking appropriate action
- Error logging for both software and hardware
- Installation and implementation of communications equipment using X21, KILOSTREAM, and MERCURY links
- Daily backup of data records and transfer of these records to off-site storage
- General maintenance of hardware and data wiring

Career Summary

1992–Present	Programmer	Sunstream Industries
1989–1992	System Controller	Trust Insurance
1985–1989	Senior System Analyst	Ringwood Assurance

1980–1985	Programmer, data storage and retrieval	Various

PROBLEM 20. 'I'VE HAD GAPS BETWEEN JOBS'

If the gaps include voluntary work, training or relevant experience – travel, for example – put these down as part of your skills, qualifications and achievements.

Otherwise, giving the year of employment, rather than month and year, will cover short employment gaps.

Example
Career Summary *(Change this . . .)*
Sollsbury Ltd
September 1992 to July 1993
Market Researcher

Hunt & Covey Retail
August 1991 to January 1992
Retail Assistant

Career Summary *(. . . to this)*
Sollsbury Ltd
1992 to 1993
Market Researcher

Hunt & Covey Retail
1991 to 1992
Retail Assistant

If the gaps are early on in your career history, focus attention on your current position, and very briefly summarise that period of employment:

Various
1989 to 1993
Retail and Market Research

PROBLEM 21. 'I'VE ONLY EVER HAD ONE JOB'

Make sure you cover the full range of skills you've used in that job, and include any experience gained from outside interests or voluntary work that will usefully expand your abilities.

Example
Personal Profile
A well organised, reliable secretary and receptionist with extensive knowledge of good office practice. Hardworking and trustworthy, with the ability to remain good humoured and unflappable under pressure.

Key Skills
Secretarial
- RSA III Typewriting – current speed 70 wpm
- RSA II Audio-typing – current speed 70 wpm
- RSA II Shorthand – current speed 120 wpm
- Typing all correspondence and reports
- Preparing printed labels
- Arranging, coordinating and minuting all departmental meetings

Reception
- Operating 20-line switchboard
- Directing all incoming calls, and dealing initially with all queries
- Administering incoming and outgoing mail
- Handling all enquiries at reception, including visitors and deliveries

Career History
Link Holdings Ltd.
1990 to Present
Receptionist
Secretary to Marketing Department

6

Starting Out

Whether you're leaving school, college or university, what do you put in your CV when you're just starting out?

PERSONAL STATEMENT

Without a career history to tell them what sort of interests and aptitudes you have, a potential employer can form a clearer picture of you from a well thought out personal statement.

It can be quite useful to know what you feel your positive qualities are, what you see as your main strengths at this early stage, and also an idea of the direction you hope your career will take.

You can include either a separate Personal Profile and Career Object-ive, or combine the two into a single statement.

QUALIFICATIONS

At this stage in your career, Education and Training is probably going to be one of the important sections, so cover it fully – especially if you have been doing a college or university course closely related to the sort of work that you want to do.

ACHIEVEMENTS

Highlight any special duties or responsibilities you have undertaken at school or college.

Include anything that rounds out the picture of you as a responsible and dependable individual with experience of more than just the classroom or lecture hall. Convince your future employer that you have qualities that will be useful to them in the workplace.

WORK EXPERIENCE

A prospective employer will be interested in any work experience you've had. It doesn't matter if your experience is different from the sort of work you are applying for, it will still demonstrate that you are familiar with a working environment. You can show that you appreciate the importance of punctuality, following instructions, being responsible, etc.

Your experience needn't necessarily be in paid employment. Include any voluntary work that you may have done, as well as work placements or work experience courses, especially if they are relevant to the sort of work that you wish to do.

For more ideas about the sort of qualities employers value, see the section on Desirable Qualities in Chapter 3.

Examples of CVs appear on the following pages:

1. **Richard Quinlan** – school leaver with relevant work experience
2. **Angela Walker** – school leaver with relevant skills and experience
3. **Pamela Heart** – school leaver without work experience, but with some voluntary work
4. **Anthony Dickens** – college leaver with some relevant work experience
5. **Linda Darin** – college leaver with some work experience
6. **Kevin Clarke** – graduate with excellent work experience
7. **Yolande Eden** – university graduate with some work experience.

Richard Quinlan
9 Barge's Brook Lane
Upper Tindle
Warwickshire
WR3 6VN

Tel. 0188 0000000

Personal Profile
A hard-working and dependable school leaver, with a good eye for detail, and able to work well both independently and in a team. Part-time and holiday work at a local newsagent and a soft-furnishings shop, has taught the value of punctuality, following instructions accurately, and also developed confidence in the ability to handle day-to-day problems appropriately.

With a particular interested in retail work, either sales, marketing or distribution, I would appreciate a position that provided the opportunity to continue to build further retail experience.

Education
1990–1995 City Park School
GCSEs:
- General Science B
- Maths C
- German B
- History B
- English language D

Employment
Kay News Newsagents
1993–Present
Newspaper Distributor

- Sorted deliveries
- Delivered newspapers and magazines reliably
- Handled enquiries and complaints
- Collected cash

Drum House Furnishings
Summer 1995
Sales and Store Room Assistant

- Served and assisted customers
- Maintained displays
- Took details of customer orders
- Prepared orders for distribution office

Personal Details
Date of birth: 1 February 1979
Health: Non-smoker
Interests: Acting and stage management. I belong to the local amateur dramatics club and am secretary to the Drama Youth Group.
References: Available on request

Angela Walker

31 Pollard Way
Mash Cross
Cambridge
CM14 2KL

Tel. 0164 0000000

Personal Profile:

A highly motivated school leaver with experience of office work. Punctual, reliable and willing to learn, with a good basic education and a strong aptitude for organization and administration.

Key Skills:

- Keyboard skills – 40 wpm
- Operating
  - fax machine
  - photocopiers – Canon and Rank Xerox
  - franking machine
- Preparing and writing routine correspondence
- Organising and carrying out routine administrative work
  - maintaining records
  - dealing with incoming telephone calls
  - dealing with incoming mail

Work Experience:

Summer 1995
Ashbourn & Sedley
Office Assistant

1994–1995
Marsh Cross School Administration Department
Administrative Assistant (part-time/voluntary)

Education:

1988–1995 Marsh Cross School
'O' levels:

- English language
- English literature
- Maths
- French
- History
- Economics

Introduction to Computer Literacy
RSA Stage I Keyboard Skills
RSA Stage I Office Skills

Personal Details:

Date of birth: 30 March 1977
Interests: Riding and pony-trekking, reading and cinema
References available on request

Pamela Heart
87 First Road
Impney
Hereford
HE15 6TD

Tel. 0174 0000000

Personal Profile
A friendly, outgoing person. Reliable, conscientious and happy to work both as part of a team and on own initiative.

Achievements
- Representing school in Athletics and Cross-Country Running
- Participating in City Marathon 1995
- Secretary of Under-18 Squash and Racquet team
- Elected House Captain

Education
1988–1995 Heath House King's School
'O' level:
- French B
- History C
- Maths C
- General Science C
- English language D

'A' level:
- French C
- History C

Computer skills
- Wordperfect 5.1
- Lotus 1-2-3
- Word for Windows 6.0

Voluntary Work Experience
Working with the elderly
Regularly visited four residents of local sheltered housing to help with shopping and every-day household tasks.

Holiday Playscheme
Coached under-11s in squash, badminton and tennis in groups of four or five during summer and Easter holidays.

Personal Details
Date of birth: 20 April 1977
Non-smoker

Anthony Dickens

7 Yelland Avenue
Port Nearsby
Pickering
PS12 7HG

Tel: 0134 0000000

Personal Profile	A hard working, self-motivated and responsible college graduate with an outgoing personality and excellent communication skills who enjoys meeting challenges and seeing them through, while remaining confident and good humoured under pressure. A problem-solver with the ability to adapt well to new situations and to work as an effective team member.
Career Objectives	I am looking for a position where I can made good use of, and further develop, my broad-based and thorough education in business and finance.

Education and Training

1994 to 1995   **BTEC National Diploma in Business and Finance – year 2**
Thorford College

- Administration systems
- Business environment
- Human resources
- Financial planning and control
- Elements of investment
- Innovation and change
- Business statistics
- Personnel, policies and procedures
- Insurance two

1993 to 1994   **BTEC National Diploma in Business and Finance – year 1**
Thorford College

- Principles and practice of insurance
- Elements of banking
- Accounting procedures
- Business Information Technology
- Financial resources
- Physical resources
- Marketing process

1992 to 1993	**BTEC First Diploma in Business and Finance** Eastville College of Further Education

- Insurance proficiency one
- Production
- Business Information Technology
- Administrative support
- People in business
- Business resources and procedures
- Administrative systems and procedures
- Business world

Work History

1991 to present	**Bealsway** Corington **Cashier and Kiosk Assistant** Responsibilities:

- Handled large amounts of money
- Customer care
- Alcohol and cigarette legislation

Work experience	**National Associative Bank** Corington **Lakeland Bank** Corington **Mansfield Bank** Pickering

Responsibilities:
- Carried out basic office procedures and clerical work, including filing and photocopying.
- Observed and assessed departmental procedures including:
  — Foreign exchange
  — Mortgage and lending
  — Pensions
  — High risk accounts
  — Customer services
  — Processing room

Additional skills	**Computer skills:** Word Perfect 5.1 Familiarity with Windows environment, and use of spreadsheets and databases.
Personal	Date of birth: 18 May 1975
Interests	I enjoy riding and swimming, and support my local football and basketball teams. I also enjoy listening to music.
References	Available on request

Linda Darin
34 Southernwood Drive
Hendy Hill
Edgerton
Surrey SR21 9AS

Tel. 0000 0000000

Personal Profile
A highly motivated college leaver with work experience, I am competent and reliable, with a good eye for detail. My experience of working with the public has taught me the value of friendliness, open-mindedness and of having a good sense of humour, as well as how to communicate effectively at all levels. It has also given me confidence in my ability to handle day-to-day problems appropriately.

I have recently completed a BTEC National Diploma in Travel and Tourism, and would appreciate a position that provided the opportunity to continue to build further experience in this area.

Employment
Hall Dean Markets
1992–1993
Sales Assistant
- Served and assisted customers
- Handled cash
- Dealt with enquiries and complaints

Voluntary Work Experience
- Raised funds for CCRF (Childhood Cancer Relief Fund)
- Worked with children with learning difficulties

Education and Training
1993–1995 Edgerton College
BTEC National Diploma in Travel and Tourism
The course covered all aspects of travel and tourism, including:
- World-wide travel geography
- Airport operations
- Resort representatives
- Finance
- Travel services

Language Skills:
- Spanish
- Italian
- German
- French

Computer Skills:
- Word Perfect 5.1
- Windows experience

1987–1993 Edgerton School
'O' levels:
Five including Maths and English
Services to Business
Services to People

Personal Details

Date of birth:	19 July 1976
Licence:	Full, clean, UK driving licence
Interests:	Member of: Edgerton hockey club Edgerton athletics club Southland athletics club Affiliated to the BSJA (horse riding)
References:	Available on request

Kevin Clarke
16 Whiteside Gardens,
Kesdale,
Lincs, LN5 7TU

(0132) 0000000

Personal Profile

Biological Sciences graduate with first-hand laboratory and administrative experience in an industrial environment and an understanding of the requirements of a commercial organisation. Quick to learn and used to adapting to high pressure and tight deadlines while remaining both good humoured and accurate.

Work Experience

Summer 1994
Dale Chemicals
Laboratory Assistant:

- Responsible for trials of chemical scrubbing techniques
- Administered trial process
- Analysed data and prepared reports accordingly

Summer 1993
Seabright Pharmaceuticals
General Assistant:

- Coordinated administration of full-scale drug trials
- Responsible for data collation requiring 100% accuracy
- Prepared interim reports
- Carried out administrative requirements of the department

Education

1992–1995	University of the North	
	BSc (Hons) Biological Sciences – 2(ii)	
1985–1992	Kesdale High School	
	'O' levels	Seven 'O' levels including Maths and English
	'A' levels	Maths, Chemistry, Biology
Computer Literacy:	Wordperfect 5.1	
	Lotus 1-2-3	
Languages:	Conversational French	

Personal Details

Date of birth	15 November 1974
Interests	Reading, swimming, music
References	Available on request

Yolande Eden
77 Terrence Place
Long Common
Cheshire
CH15 8SX

Tel. (0194) 0000000

Career Objective

A Computer Science graduate with a keen interest in practical applications and information systems, seeking a career where a background in problem solving would be an advantage.

Education

1992–1995

Year 3

BSc Computer Science
West Midlands University

- **Robotics:**
  concepts
  VAL
  3-D modelling of
  components
  assembly
  matrices
- **Graphics:**
  2-D and 3-D
  projection
  transformation matrices
- **Communications:**
  network theory
  protocols
  hardware

- **Database Theory:**
  structure
  storage
  design
- **Formal Logic:**
  trinary
  fuzzy
  temporal
- **Artificial Intelligence:**
  Popll
  expert systems
  Prolog
  theory of neural nets

Final Year Project:
The Use of Geographical Information Systems. The project was to write a geographical database which, using a GIS package, could plot NHS patient data for the West Midlands. Project included use of OS map data. Package used:
Arc-Info under X-Windows on a DEC workstation

Year 2

- **Computer Science:**
  database design with
  SSADM
  Ad programming
  micro-electronics
  formal logic
  software design methods

- **Maths:**
  transformation
  matrices with
  coordinate systems
  multiple differentiation
  integration

Year 1
- **Computer Science:**
  software management
  programming
  methodologies
  micro-electronics
  programming in Ada

- **Maths:**
  graphs and matrices
  complex equations
  differential equations
  integration with
  trigonometric
  functions

Key Skills:

- **Programming languages:**
  - Ada
  - Pascal
  - Popll
  - Prolog
  - VAL
  - SML
  - C
  - Modula 2
  - Clipper 5
  - ArcInfo
- **Environments:**
  - Sunview
  - X-Windows
  - MS-Windows
  - Apple Mac
  - UNIX
  - MSDOS

Work Experience:

Summer 1994
Tripp Electronics
Littledean
Administrative Assistant

Summer 1993
Torrington Newcombe
Olstead
Clerical Assistant

Summer 1992
Tripp Electronics
Littledean
Clerk

Personal:

Date of birth: 19 January 1974
Full, clean, UK driving licence

Interests:

I am an active member of the University Irish Folk Club and enjoy music, listening and performing, and dancing. I also enjoy cycling and swimming.

References:

Available on request

7

Starting again

At some time in your life, you may find yourself re-entering the job market after a break. This can be for a number of reasons: bringing up a family, taking time out for travel or voluntary work, or redundancy or unemployment.

Don't apologise for your career break. Gaps in employment, for whatever reason, are a fact of life and should be handled positively and assertively.

Emphasise your relevant experience and concentrate on your skills and qualities. Draw attention to what you have done, rather than what you haven't.

CAREER OBJECTIVE

You may be returning to a different type of job from the one that you used to do. If so, a Career Objective at the top of the page can be useful. Use it to connect the three parts of your working life – your previous employment, your experience during the break, and your future direction.

KEY SKILLS

Highlight your key skills, achievements or qualifications. Include any gained through voluntary or part-time work during your career break. Include, too, qualifications and skills gained through education or training, and mention any ways in which you have kept abreast of developments in your trade or profession.

You might like to add positive ways in which you have changed: increased maturity, for example, or more responsibility, confidence, understanding, new skills, insight, etc.

CAREER HISTORY

What have you done during your break?

Depending on how long you have been out of employment, things may have changed a lot since you last worked. Employers sometimes worry about returners being out of date with what's happening in the industry. They may wonder if you will be willing to adapt to new ways of doing things, or if you will stick to the ways that you already know.

Point out how you have kept up your skills, and mention anything that you have done to improve or up-date them. Any training you have done during this time will be a useful indicator of your interest and motivation. It's not a bad idea, in any case, to go back to the workplace better qualified than when you left it.

Include all the work experience you have had during your career break, including voluntary work, part-time work, special responsibilities and duties, etc. Even if it was unpaid, an employer will still be interested in what you have done recently.

Examples of CVs appear on the following pages:

1. **Janet Sandiman** – returning after child-care, looking for a career change after training
2. **Ananda Vires** – returning after child-care, voluntary work experience
3. **Daniel Guys** – returning to full-time work after extensive travelling
4. **Edward Kingsman** – returning after redundancy with further training and related voluntary work
5. **Diane Walker** – returning after redundancy with updated training.

JANET SANDIMAN
14 Eastover Common
Oxhill
Avon
AV20 4CP

Tel. 0100 0000000

Career Objective

A mature and responsible individual with counselling skills and broad experience of nursing and caring for others, now looking for the opportunity to work with clients and assist them to explore their concerns, focus on underlying issues, and consider options towards setting and achieving goals.

Key Skills

- Encouraging and motivating others
- Providing counselling support for trauma and bereavement
- Preparing others for, and supporting them through, life changes
- An understanding of women's health issues
- Computer literate

Key Qualifications

- State Enrolled Nurse
- Certificate of Counselling Theory AEB/CAC
- Certificate of Counselling Practice AEB/CAC
- Open Access vocational training in:
  — Post-Trauma Stress and Critical Incident Debriefing
  — Primary Health Care Counselling
  — Managing Short-Term Counselling Work within Primary Care
  — Women and Mental Health

Career History

1988–Present
Responsible for the full-time care of my two children, now at school, while also undergoing training as a counsellor.

Leigh House Hospital
1985–1988

State Enrolled Nurse

Responsible for medical and surgical patients:

- Prepared patients physically and mentally for surgery
- Provided patient care post-surgery
- Supported and counselled relatives of terminal patients
- Assisted on ward rounds
- Updated patient records
- Administered drugs
- Dealt with enquiries from patients and their families

Eastern Hospital
1981–1985
State Enrolled Nurse
Responsible for day-to-day working in out-patients department:
- Supported patients and provided patient care
- Assisted with routine procedures
- Dealt with enquiries from patients and their families
- Prepared working areas
- Compiled patient records

Education and Training
1990–1992 Westbrook College of Further Education
        Certificate of Counselling Theory AEB/CAC
        Certificate of Counselling Practice AEB/CAC

1991–1994 Oxhill Community College
        Open Access vocational courses:
- Post-Trauma Stress and Critical Incident Debriefing
- Primary Health Care Counselling
- Managing Short-Term Counselling Work within Primary Care
- Women and Mental Health

1979–1981 Langport Hospital
        Student Nurse for State Enrolled Nurse

1974–1979 St. Lawrence School for Girls
        Six 'O' levels including Maths, English, Chemistry and Biology

Personal Details
Date of birth:	9 July 1963
Licence:	Full, clean UK driving licence, own car
Interests:	Computers, education, active member of the Oxhill community volunteers group
References:	Available on request

Ananda Vires

2 Gorstan Mead
Matley
North Yorkshire
NY19 7DC

Tel. 0100 0000000

Personal Profile:

A reliable, conscientious and efficient computer-literate administrator with good secretarial and organisational skills. Proficient at working both on own initiative and as part of a team.

Key Skills:

- Secretarial, including word-processing
  — Word 6 for Windows
  — Wordperfect 5.1
  — Microsoft Office
- Excellent telephone manner
- Resourceful, reliable team member

Career History

1991–Ongoing
Matley North End Residents Association
Secretary
Organised and administered voluntary Tenants Association:
- Organised monthly meetings and Annual General meetings
- Wrote, typed and circulated minutes
- Dealt with correspondence
- Liaised with Housing Office
- Drafted reports on specific issues as member of various working parties
- Represented Association at meetings of other organisations, the Tenants Forum and special interest groups

1987–Present
During this period I have also been caring for my three children full-time.

1982–1987
Benn, Hodge and Keen
Secretary
Responsible for secretarial support to department:
- Typed reports and correspondence
- Organised appointments and arranged meetings
- Minuted all departmental meetings
- Responded to telephone enquiries and requests
- Coordinated department work schedule.

1977–1982
Coburg & Partners
Secretary/clerk
Organised and carried out routine office administration, maintained records and files, dealt with incoming mail, prepared routine correspondence

Education:

1994–1995
Community Open College
Computer Literacy (CLAIT) Stages I & II
Introduction to Information Technology
RSA Stage I Office Skills

1970–1977
Holm Place School
'O' levels:
Seven including Maths and English
'A' levels:
- English language
- English literature
- French

Personal Details:

Date of birth: 10 March 1959
Interests: Badminton, swimming
Car owner/driver with full, clean UK licence
References available on request

Daniel Guys
68 St John's Road
Adrington
Sussex
SX4 2JN

Tel. 0100 0000000

Career Objective
A graduate with first-rate language skills gained through both formal study and extensive travel, as well as teaching English as a Foreign Language in Europe.
The position sought is one that will allow me to use my experience and abilities to good effect in a forward thinking, Europe-orientated organisation.

Key Skills:
Languages:
- Fluent written and spoken French
  — Conversational
  — Business
  — Literary
- Excellent Business and Conversational Spanish

Tuition:
- Teaching Business English to Spanish business people in on-site training programmes
- Teaching Adult Education classes in France
- Teaching student groups in Swedish summer school

Other:
- Computer literate, including word-processing packages and spread-sheets
- Experienced in meeting deadlines, dealing with clients, office procedures, and compiling records

Work Experience:
1991–1995
Travelling in Africa, Asia and Europe
Teacher of English as a Foreign Language
Responsible for teaching English to a variety of students:
- Delivered teaching programmes to several professional companies
- Taught Business English at all levels from students to company directors
- Devised and taught mixed ability adult evening class
- Encouraged and motivated students
- Organised leisure activities for multilingual groups of students at residential summer school

1989–1991
Torrington Ellis Ltd
Claims Supervisor
Initially employed as a graduate clerk/trainee, I was promoted to Claims Supervisor:
- Dealt with telephone enquiries and correspondence
- Processed claims
- Issued cheques
- Ensured deadlines were kept
- Prepared claims

Education:

1992
South East College
RSA Certificate
Teaching English as a Foreign Language

1986–1989
University of East Midlands
BA Hons 2:1
French Language and Literature

1979–1986
Fairchurch Secondary School
'O' levels:
Seven including Maths and English
'A' levels:
- English literature
- French
- History

Personal Details:

Date of birth: 10 August 1968
Interests: Foreign cinema, food and cookery, hill-walking
Health: Non-smoker
Prepared to relocate
References available on request

Edward Kingsman
The Firs
8 Langport Road
Coveringham
Lincoln
LN12 2JH

Tel. 0100 0000000

Personal Profile

A skilled engineer with both practical and managerial skills, gained through many years experience of supervising staff including apprentices and trainees. An outgoing, down-to-earth person who enjoys being involved with whatever is going on, and has encountered and solved many problems with both machines and people.

Key Skills

- Managing staff in a high turnover production environment
- Providing a first-rate engineering service to internal and external customers
- Project management and budget preparation
- Training and motivating staff
- Computer literate

Career History

JMF Training Consortium
1995–Present
Training Supervisor
Trained Community Project volunteers in basic engineering skills for a variety of projects including environmental and conservation work.

G&T Tower Ltd
1987–1994
Industrial Engineer
Responsible for all industrial engineering services at factory and divisional level. Monitored, coordinated and delivered production engineering service with particular emphasis on product costing, value engineering, pre-production engineering and methods improvement. Provided work measurement facilities and maintained bonus scheme.

APT Engineering Ltd
1980–1987
Director/Partner
Planned, organised and implemented all aspects of running a small engineering company.

Pearl Valves Ltd.
1975–1980
Foreman Supervisor
Managed day-to-day control of production lines on a two-shift system. Supervised leading hands, setters and operatives, production planning, quality assurance, coordination of tools and materials and bonus scheme administration.
Promoted to position after joining company in 1973.

Education and Training

1995 CRO Training Services
City & Guilds Training for Trainers Certificate

1993 Open University
The Effective Manager

1973–1975 Keyfield College
City & Guilds Certificate in Mechanical Engineering

North East College
Supplementary certificates:
- Toolroom Practices
- Inspection and Quality Assurances
- Health and Safety Planning

In-work training
Internal and external courses:
- Accountancy Part I & II
- Team management skills
- Negotiation skills
- Computer Smartware II
- Spreadsheets
- Word-processing

Personal Details

Date of birth: 9 March 1955
Licence: Full, clean, UK driving licence, advanced motorist's certificate
Interests: Computers and computing, conservation (I am a member of the local environmental and conservation group) current affairs, swimming.
References: Available on request

DIANE WALKER
83 Draycot Place,
Eastley, Surrey SR1 2AA
Telephone: 0000 0000000

Personal Profile

An experienced administrator and office manager with an extensive knowledge of business practices especially in accounting, bookkeeping, and inventory control.

A good communicator, who has demonstrated a high degree of initiative and self-motivation, and enjoys the challenge of a busy, demanding work environment. Conscientious, with the ability to maintain a consistently high standard of work under pressure. A good team member and leader.

Key Skills

- Supervising staff
- Implementing standard procedures accurately
- Prioritising workload
- Analysing and rectifying errors
- Conversational French
- Computer Skills:
  - Word for Windows
  - Lotus Works
  - SuperCalc

Career History

1994–present   Eastley Training Centre
NVQ level 3 Clerical Skills Course
Administration and Supervision. Advanced course to update and expand office management skills

1985–1993   Friends Assurance Association
Office Administrator
Responsible for all documentation and records. Also dealt with queries, and the organisation of data within the department

1981–1985   Keyline Retail
Section Manager
Supervised staff and attended to customers in busy city centre store. Responsible for daily administration of section including stock control, turn-over, and complaints

1977–1981	Scottish Finance Co.
	Office Administrator
	Analysed and rectified accounting errors in customer accounts

1974–1977	United Insurance Ltd
	Office Administrator
	Carried out administrative work of department including invoicing and ordering. Processed payroll and coordinated work schedules

Education and Training

1993–present	Eastley Training Centre
	NVQ level 3
	Clerical Skills Course concentrating on administration and supervision. This advanced course updates and expands my current office management skills, and also covers Information Technology.

1974–1975	Oldbarrow College of Further Education
	College Secretarial Diploma

1967–1974	Impney Court School
	'O' levels: seven, including Maths and English
	'A' levels: French, English, Economics

Personal Details

Date of birth:	12 December 1956
Health:	Non-smoker
Driving:	Full, clean, UK licence
Interests:	I work as a dresser for charity fashion shows on a freelance basis at evenings and weekends. This involves being able to keep to a tight timetable, work quickly and accurately and remain cool, calm and collected under extreme pressure.
References:	Available on request

8

Keeping Going

Employers' attitudes *are* changing, but, if you are 45 or over, you may wonder how to present yourself in the best light so as to maximise your employment and promotion chances.

Concentrate on the positives. Employers perceive older workers as stable and reliable, mature in their approach, and with good interpersonal skills. Many young people have these qualities too, of course. But one thing older people can offer that younger people may not be able to, is experience.

How can you emphasise your experience without filling your CV with a long list of previous jobs?

CAREER PROFILE

Summarise your career path in a Career Profile at the top of your CV. This can speak more fully and persuasively for you than a list of job titles in your Career History section.

KEY EXPERIENCE

Rather than a Key Skills or Qualifications section, consider including a Key Experience section instead. This will clearly emphasise what could be one of your strongest selling points.

ACHIEVEMENTS

Demonstrate that your experience brings results and that you have the track record to prove it. Your key achievements can be combined with your Key Experience, put in a separate section, or clearly listed under your Career History.

CAREER HISTORY

Concentrate on your most recent jobs and edit the rest ruthlessly. For early work, consider simply listing jobs and job-titles, and/or grouping jobs together under the heading 'Various'.

PERSONAL DETAILS

There is no law that says you *must* include your date of birth on your CV, and it is up to you whether you include it or not.

However, by the time a reader reaches this final section, they should have formed a positive impression of you that will persuade them to consider your application whatever your age.

Examples of CVs appear on the following pages:

1. **Valerie David** – continuing as a project manager
2. **Dominic Hoy** – continuing as an electrical engineer
3. **Alan Bevan** – continuing voluntary work after retirement.

VALERIE DAVID
17 Three Elms Field
Garby
Stourling
HU21 5GN
Tel. 0000 0000000 (home)
00000000000 (work)

Career Profile
A highly trained, confident and effective **project manager** with significant experience
in a broad range of construction, manufacturing and industrial projects and proven
skills in exploring, designing and implementing solutions and the management of
change.

Key Experience
- Ten years experience in project management working in a wide range of environments
- Knowledge of health and safety and employment legislation and practice
- An understanding of staff motivation and training
- A clear commitment to excellence
- An established track record in effective solutions

Career History
1985 to Present
Bell and Dutton Consultants

Project Manager
Actively managed a number of projects, including:

Dann Environmental Ltd
Project – Resources and Traffic
Managed traffic flow and resource during development of existing sites and
establishment of new 20 acre industrial site:

- Liaised with external consultants
- Gathered, verified and analysed traffic flow data
- Maintained information flow between departments

Revised site layout and traffic handling patterns resulting in:

- Expansion and full use of most effective areas
- Elimination of single deliveries in favour of multiple stock drops
- Improved vehicle safety

Whitby Transport Group
Project – Storage and Stock Handling
Developed and improved stock storage and handling system:

- Researched safety regulations
- Devised simplified visual verification system
- Designed and oversaw implementation of new system

Devised and implemented introduction of new storage systems resulting in:

- Improved stock handling and rotation
- Reduced stock holding
- Safer working practices
- Improved storage facility of flammable and explosive material

1977 to 1985
The Industrial Training Group Ltd
Training Manager
Managed and administered training projects for agency serving up to 50 local engineering companies:

- Researched opportunities for improvement in services to clients
- Determined supervisory management training needs

Produced comprehensive analysis of training opportunities, skills gaps and information management systems resulting in:

- Fully costed training scheme and syllabus
- Effective development and expansion of training group

Pre 1977
Various
Management and Administrative
A range of managerial and administrative positions for various companies. Responsibilities and achievements over this period include:

- Ensured safe operation of chemical plant during site development
- Increased production turnover of organics at agrochemical company
- Served on safety and work practices committee
- Contributed to operations manual
- Instituted new management control and information systems

Education and Training
MBA
Southern School of Business

Diploma in Supervisory Management
Diploma in Operations Management
Cork West College

Computer skills:
— CLAIT Certificate in computer literacy
— Excel
— Minitab
— Ami Pro 3.1
— Harvard Graphics

Personal Details
Date of birth   8 September 1944

Interests   Environmental issues
        Wildlife and wildlife photography

Health: Non-smoker

Car owner/driver with full, clean, UK licence

References available on request

Dominic Hoy
4 Clements Avenue
High Cross
Berkshire
BK17 5LM

Tel. 0000 0000000

Career Profile
A skilled and experienced electrical engineer, expert in all aspects of installation, servicing and repair, together with an understanding of staff supervision and management gained in a variety of environments.

Key Skills and Experience

- Ten years' experience in electrical engineering
- Knowledge of installing, servicing and repairing electro-mechanical and electronic equipment
- An understanding of precision instrumentation
- An established track record in staff supervision
- A clear commitment to high standards

Career History
1987 to Present
Caversham Electrical Engineering
Section Supervisor
Electrical Fitter
Worked in measurement division and repair shop:

- Repaired electronic and electro-mechanical equipment
- Performed or verified precision instrument calibration
- Supervised, administered, and coordinated ten full-time and three part-time staff
- Planned work schedules
- Maintained work-sheet records
- Oversaw apprentice training
- Ensured excellent standard of department maintained
- Promoted to Supervisor in 1989

1976 to 1987
Scouts Engineering
Electrical Maintenance Engineer
Worked in maintenance shop and with overhead cranes and hoists:

- Repaired high speed machine tools
- Serviced overhead equipment
- Overhauled and maintained equipment
- Maintained control equipment
- Performed general electrical maintenance on the site
- Maintained high standards within tight deadlines

Prior to 1976
Various
Electrical engineer
Responsible for electrical engineering and maintenance in a variety of situations including early experience with electronics and some communications.

Completed apprenticeship in electrical engineering with Abbott Engineering.

Education and Training

City and Guilds
Electrical Engineering

Specialist training courses:
- Control equipment for high speed tools
- Precision instrument calibration and maintenance

Personal Details

Date of birth   16 May 1949

Interests   Sailing
                     Studying for Costal Navigation Certificate
                     Swimming

Health: Non-smoker

Car owner/driver with full, clean, UK licence

References available on request

Alan Bevan

50 April Way
Whitpool
Kent
KT3 6ZP

Tel. 0000 0000000 (answer phone)

Career Objective

A professional human resources officer with a fundamental interest in workplace equality together with practical experience of helping young people and those with physical disabilities into rewarding and satisfying employment. Keen to continue using these skills and expertise for the benefit of the community.

Key Skills and Experience

- Considerable experience in all aspects of human resource assessment and development
- Highly evolved skills in personnel management
- Extensive contacts within training agencies, Training and Enterprise Councils, and employers
- Qualified and experienced in the use of psychometric and aptitude testing
- Experienced in devising, delivering and assessing training courses
- Thorough knowledge of employment law

Career History

1995 to Present
Life Line
Voluntary helper

- Set up and administered career advice and job search service for young people with physical handicaps
- Represented Life Line at the Business Network Forum to promote equality in the workplace
- Liaised with local TEC and FEFC for education and training opportunities and funding

1988 to Present
Perryman Goldley
Human Resources Manager

- Overall personnel function for office and general staff
- Developed personnel policies and procedures for financial group
- Improved effectiveness of human resource development strategies
- Managed introduction of performance evaluation system

1977 to 1988
Terrence Parnell Co. Ltd
Personnel Officer

- Complete personnel function for Head Office and Southern Region Staff
- Administered records, pay and contractual documents
- Promoted from assistant personnel officer in 1980

1967 to 1977
Fleet Industrial
Personnel Assistant
Clerical Officer
Clerical Assistant

Previous clerical and administrative experience gained in a variety of roles between leaving Fieldhouse College and joining Fleet Industrial.

Education and training
Fellow of the Institute of Personnel and Development

Diploma in Personnel Management
Lincoln Business School

Diploma in Education
Fieldhouse College
Work related training:
— Psychometric testing
— Aptitude testing
— Assessment skills
— Careers guidance and counselling

Personal Details
Date of birth   14 March 1936

Interests   Photography
                Fell-walking – active member and secretary of Sindon Lake Walkers' Club

Car owner/driver with full, clean, UK licence

References available on request

9

CVs for Practical Jobs

Organisations depend on trustworthy people doing practical jobs reliably. If jobs such as building maintenance, security, deliveries, etc are not done accurately, effectively and efficiently, other employees will be prevented from carrying out their own work.

A prospective employer reading your CV wants to know that you'll be able to do the job competently and skilfully. Demonstrate clearly that you know what needs to be done and that you know how to do it.

The most important areas to emphasise are your past experience, along with any recognised training you have in this particular skill. These will be a good indication of your ability to perform well in the future.

The key qualities needed for most practical jobs are:

- Knowledge and hands-on experience of the job
- These days, usually, proof of adequate training such as NVQ or City and Guilds qualifications
- Competence and reliability
- Self reliance *as well as* the ability to follow instructions accurately
- Flexibility.

What will help to get these points across?

CAREER PROFILE

An idea of the work you have done in the past, the amount of experience you have had, and your current position, will all be useful information to a potential employer.

If you have personal qualities that are useful in your job, such as patience or confidence in dealing with the public, mention these as well.

KEY SKILLS

You may need specific qualifications for some types of practical work – an HGV licence for some sorts of driving, or a Hygiene Certificate for catering jobs. If you have relevant qualifications, put them in this section where they can be clearly seen.

Concentrate too on the practical skills that you need for your job and which have proved useful in the past. Make it clear that you understand what the job requires.

CAREER HISTORY

Emphasise the experience you have gained in each job, and the skills you have developed through doing it. Mention any specific responsibilities you have had.

The examples on the following pages show an outline CV, and CVs which make use of some or all of the above points:

1. **Outline CV**
2. **Mary Weber** – Chef
3. **Robert Morgan** – Driver
4. **Diane Donnelly** – Dental Hygienist
5. **Peter Ruckerby** – Maintenance Worker
6. **Paul Colston** – Warehouse Supervisor.

(**Your Name** in large, bold type)
(Your full address)

_____

_____

_____

(Postcode)

(Telephone number, including area code)

Career Profile

(A brief, business-like description of yourself)

(Skills)

(Experience)

(Personal strengths)

Key Skills

* (The main skills you have got)
* (Particularly those appropriate to the job you are applying for)
* _____
* _____
* _____

Career History

(**Name of Company**, usually starting with the most recent)

(Dates you worked there)

(Job title)

(Brief description of what you did)

(Brief description of what you achieved in this position)

* _____
* _____
* _____

(**Name of Company**, usually starting with the most recent)

(Dates you worked there)

(Job title)

(Brief description of what you did)

(Brief description of what you achieved in this position)

* _____
* _____
* _____

(**Name of Company**, usually starting with the most recent)

(Dates you worked there)

(Job title)

(Brief description of what you did. Jobs you did some years ago require less detail than do your more recent ones)

Education and Training

(Starting with the highest, most recent OR most relevant qualification)

(**Name of school, college, or university**)

(Dates you attended)

(The qualification you achieved)

(You could include brief details of what was covered in the course, especially if recently qualified)

-
-
-

(**Name of school, college, or university**)

(Dates you attended)

(The qualification you achieved)

(**Name of school, college, or university**)

(Dates you attended)

(The qualification you achieved)

(Don't go back further than your senior or secondary school)

(**Professional Training**)

(Details of any professional training undertaken at work)

- (Qualification or skill achieved)
-
-
-

Personal Details

(Date of birth)

(Driving licence)

(Married or single – only if relevant)

(Nationality – only if relevant)

(Interests and activities. Brief details)

(References – usually 'available on request')

Mary Weber

16 Woodland Road
Little Hadby
Norfolk
NF14 9MT

Tel. 0000 0000000

Career Profile:

A thoroughly trained, commercially minded chef with experience in large kitchens providing a high standard of quality service. A team member with good communication skills and a sound working knowledge of good health and safety practice, ready, willing and able to play a hands-on role in a demanding environment.

Key Skills:

- City & Guilds 706 1 & 2
- Intermediate Food Hygiene Certificate
- Thorough understanding of health and safety regulations
- Knowledge of chilled meals production
- Experience of therapeutic diet preparation

Career History:

St Edwards District Health Care Trust
1993–Present
Chef
Worked as member of team providing full meals service within central kitchen preparation unit for large hospital trust producing 5,000 meals a day:

- Prepared meals for consumption within the Trust and other hospitals and day centres
- Supervised routine food preparation
- Prepared food with regard to special dietary requirements such as diabetic, low salt, low fat, gluten free, etc
- Undertook preparation of food for chilling and distribution
- Packed and presented food effectively and attractively

SSB Resources South East
1987 to 1993
Chef
Assistant Chef
Provided high quality catering service to staff and visitors for a number of large commercial clients, working both on own initiative and as part of a team:

- Prepared breakfast and lunch for up to 2,500 people per day
- Undertook pastry and some confectionery work
- Delivered hospitality service requiring exceptionally high standards of preparation and presentation

Five Mile Hill School
1985 to 1987
Assistant Canteen Cook
Assisted preparation of lunch-time meals service for 1,750 children and staff including menu choices and food prepared to special requirements

Education and Training:

Norfolk City College (day release)
- City & Guilds 706 Cookery For The Catering Industry Part II
- Intermediate Food Hygiene Certificate

South Eastern College of Technology
- City & Guilds 706 Cookery For The Catering Industry Part I

St Edwards and District Secondary School
- Six 'O' levels including English and Maths

Personal Details:

Date of birth: 21 February 1965
Health: Non-smoker
Interests: All aspects of conservation – National Trust
World Wide Fund for
Nature
RSPB

References available on request

Robert Morgan
Flat 1
Riverside Court
Chiderton
Northumberland
NB14 5FL

Tel. 0000 0000000

Career Profile:
A capable, professional delivery and PCV driver, with an excellent driving record and experience of organising own round. Fully responsible for planning and delivery on own route, as well as proficient at dealing with the public in a confident and friendly manner.

Key Skills:
- Clean current UK driving licence
- PCV licence
- Thorough knowledge of the North East area
- Passenger carrying and multi-drop experience
- Able to plan and prioritise schedules and routes as well as work to instruction
- Smart appearance
- Punctual, healthy, reliable

Career History:
Bourne & Thomas Ltd
1994 to Present
Delivery Driver
- Planned and carried out multi-drop deliveries
- Collected confidential waste safely
- Transported technical products securely and competently
- Planned and organised daily and weekly schedules in agreement with team of drivers
- Maintained schedules and timetables punctually and reliably

NE Central Healthcare Trust
1990–1994
Patient Services Transport Driver
- Provided driver support for Ring and Ride scheme
- Covered two district hospital outpatient departments, three clinics and three day centres
- Arranged most efficient patient pick-up routes in association with Assistant Transport Controller
- Collected outpatients from home and took to destination
- Assisted special needs patients on and off vehicle

Pescod Foods Ltd
1987 to 1990
Customer Service Driver
- Delivered products in North East area
- Loaded van following order sheet
- Maintained delivery records and logs
- Worked flexible shift system

Various
1985–1987
Provided temporary and emergency cover for general driving and delivery work for agencies.

Education and Training:

J&B Training (for NE Central Health Trust)
Passenger Carrying Vehicle Licence

Allerton Secondary School
Four 'O' levels including Maths and English

Personal Details:

Date of birth:	6 April 1969
Interests:	Jazz and music in general
	Fell-walking
	Railway and transport enthusiast
Health:	Non-smoker
References:	Available on request

DIANE DONNELLY
Flat 1
121 East Hadbrook Gardens
London
NW12 5TT

Tel: 0000 0000000

Career Profile

A competent, reliable dental hygienist experienced in preventative dental care, with excellent interpersonal skills and a clear understanding of the place of oral hygiene in maintaining dental health. A confident, personable individual with experience of working in both private practice and a busy health centre, capable of making a significant contribution to any practice.

Key Skills

- Assessing patient dental health
- Instructing patients on dental health care
- Demonstrating oral hygiene techniques
- Removing tartar, calculus and plaque
- Effecting preventative dental care procedures such as fissure and pit sealing
- Taking and developing dental x-rays
- Administering local anaesthesia
- Providing temporary dressings
- Removing stitches following dental surgery

Key Qualifications and Experience

- Diploma Dental Hygiene
- Certificate of Proficiency in Dental Nursing

Career Summary

The Penn Clinic
1992 to Present
Dental Hygienist

Brittain, Rayne and Folks
1990 to 1992
Dental Hygienist

Portway Partners
1985 to 1989
Dental Nurse

Topwell Health Centre
1984 to 1985
Dental Receptionist

Education and Training

City Central Dental Hospital
- 1990 – Diploma of Dental Hygiene
- 1987 – Certificate of Proficiency in Dental Nursing

St James Secondary School
'O' levels:
Five including English and Human Biology

Personal Details

Date of birth:	17 October 1968
Health:	Non-smoker
Licence:	Full, clean, UK driver's licence
Interests:	Theatre and cinema
References:	Available on request

Peter Ruckerby
4 Tiverton Lane
Cresslow Common
Buckinghamshire
BK7 2WW

Tel: 0000 0000000

Career Profile

A versatile, reliable groundsworker, gardener and maintenance operative with experience of delivering professional maintenance services for first-class contractors. Proficient at planning own schedules and working on own initiative as well as being able to follow instructions accurately. Hardworking and trustworthy, with the proven ability to remain good humoured and unflappable under pressure.

Key Skills

- Institute of Groundsmanship Qualified
- Five years' experience with established maintenance company
- Experience of recreational and sports grounds maintenance
- Full clean UK driving licence
- Able to work 'on call' rota

Career History

1991 to Present
Cornwallis Building & Maintenance Contractors
Maintenance Operative
Provided a top quality maintenance service to a variety of clients in the Buckinghamshire area.
Work undertaken included:
- Basic daily maintenance and preventative repair of properties
- Routine building improvements and repairs
- Carpentry
- Painting and decorating
- Completed service and maintenance logs for each site

Groundsman
Carried out grounds maintenance for two sites
Work undertaken included:
- General seasonal maintenance of grounds
- Maintenance duties:
  - Mowing, rolling and marking
  - Use of pesticides and fertilisers
  - Use of machinery, tools and plant
  - Use of ride-on and gang mower
- Horticultural duties
  - Tree and shrub planting and pruning
  - Turfing
  - Propagating, planting and plant husbandry

1987 to 1991
South Berkshire and District Leisure Department
Groundsworker Manual 3

1983 to 1987
Hayes & Heartcliffe Environmental Services
Groundsworker Manual 1

Education and Training

North Buckinghamshire College of Education
Institute of Groundsmanship: National Practical Certificate

1975–1980 Clevedon School
'O' levels:
Five including Maths and English

Personal Details

Date of birth: 18 January 1964

Health: Non-smoker

Interests: Squash, swimming.
                 Member of the local rugby team

Licence: Full, clean UK driver's licence

References: Available on request

Paul Colston
71 Upper East Gate
Hadworth
York
YK7 4DP

Tel. 0000 0000000

Personal Profile:

A logical and methodical warehouse supervisor with an excellent health and safety record and experience of both warehousing and counter service. An adaptable team worker also willing and able to take responsibility for efficient team productivity.

Key Skills:

Experienced in all aspects of receiving, storing, retrieving and sending out goods:

- Supervising up to 15 staff and checking goods in and out
- Arranging most efficient use of storage locations
- Order picking and assembling:
  - working from order sheets
  - noting inconsistencies
  - checking state of stock
  - re-ordering as necessary
- Packing and dispatching:
  - assembling orders
  - preparing for transport – postage or delivery
- Store-keeping:
  - selling parts as trade counter assistant
  - maintaining computerized record system
  - using computer terminal and checking printouts to assess availability of parts
- NVQ level 2 – Wholesaling, Warehousing and Stores

Career Summary:

Auto City Supplies Ltd
1991 to Present
Warehouse Supervisor
Warehouse Worker

Northern Stores Ltd
1987 to 1991
Warehouse Worker

H Pearson McDuff
1985 to 1987
Warehouse Worker
Shelf Stacker

Various
1984 to 1985
Shelf Stacker
General Assistant

Education and Training:

South Yorkshire College (day release)
- NVQ level 2 - Wholesaling, Warehousing and Stores
- NVQ level 1 - Wholesaling, Warehousing and Stores

Edmund Fairview School
- Six 'O' levels, including Maths

Personal Details:

Date of birth: 9 June 1968

Licence: Full, clean, UK driver's licence

Interests: All team sports. Captain of Hadworth and District Cricket Team

References available on request

10

CVs for Creative Jobs

Creative people provide solutions to problems.

It's the creative person's job to use their technical skill and expertise – whether in design, graphics, engineering or whatever – to achieve tangible results with originality and flair.

Most creative vacancies will require evidence of your creative skills by way of a portfolio of examples. It's important that your CV puts these creative skills in context and emphasises your ability to deliver work of a similar quality, reliably and professionally. The most important area to emphasise, therefore, is your past experience of doing this, which will be a good indication of your ability to do so again in the future.

The key qualities employers usually require in creative personnel are:

- A thorough understanding of your specific field
- The ability to come up with effective solutions to problems
- Competence, and dependably high standards
- The ability to work both individually *and* with a team to achieve results
- Flexibility, energy and enthusiasm.

What will get these characteristics across to a prospective employer?

CAREER PROFILE

An idea of what you have done and how you have done it will be useful in assessing your knowledge and experience

KEY EXPERIENCE

Technical and practical competence and experience are key requirements in creative jobs; it's only when they are present that style and originality can develop. Outline the range of skills you have, and expand on your achievements. This will help an employer to assess your probable future performance.

CAREER HISTORY

Your experience of encountering and solving problems is important. Give details of the skills you have developed in different jobs.

The examples on the following pages show an outline CV including a Key Experience section, and CVs which make use of some or all of the above points:

1. **Outline CV**
2. **Rosa Devon** – Interior and exhibition designer
3. **Alan Moorhouse** – Writer and broadcaster
4. **Hannah Gansa** – Editorial assistant and photographer
5. **Luke Jump** – Graphic artist
6. **Barbra Kingdom** – Video maker.

(**Your Name** in large, bold type)
(Your full address)

(Postcode)

(Telephone number, including area code)

Career Profile

(A brief description of yourself)

(Personal qualities)

(Experience)

(Creative skills and strengths)

Key Experience

- (Your main areas of experience)
- (Particularly where appropriate to the job you are applying for)
-
-
-

Career History

(**Name of Company**, usually starting with the most recent)

(Dates you worked there)

(Job title)

(Brief description of what you did)

(Brief description of what you achieved in this position)

-
-
-

(**Name of Company**)

(Dates you worked there)

(Job title)

(Brief description of what you did)

(Brief description of what you achieved in this position)

-
-
-

(**Name of Company**)

(Dates you worked there)

(Job title)

(Brief description of what you did. Jobs you did some years ago require less detail than your more recent ones)

Education and Training

(Professional Training)

(Details of any professional training undertaken at work)

- (Qualification or skill achieved)
-
-
-
-

(Membership of Professional Bodies)

(or institutes)

(Name of school, college, or university) (Starting with the highest, most recent OR most relevant qualification)

(Dates you attended)

(The qualification you achieved)

(Name of school, college, or university)

(Dates you attended)

(The qualification you achieved)

(Name of school, college, or university)

(Dates you attended)

(The qualification you achieved)

(Don't go back further than your senior or secondary school)

Personal Details

(Date of birth)

(Driving licence)

(Married or single – only if relevant)

(Nationality – only if relevant)

(Interests and activities. Brief details)

(References – usually 'available on request')

Rosa Devon

31 Verdon Villas
Spring Gate Heath
Essex EX12 7YC

Tel. 0000 0000000

Career Profile:

An experienced designer with a background in retail display and domestic design, and a sound understanding of detailed specification, planning and budgeting, and liaising with both clients and sub-contractors.

Key Experience:

- Overall management of refurbishment of specialist retail outlet, having responsibility for:
    — Design
    — Planning
    — Budgeting
    — Materials specification
    — Purchasing
    — Hiring sub-contractors
- Successfully designing and planning over two dozen shop floor and point-of-sale exhibitions for a home-furnishing retail chain
- Establishing a successful interior design service in conjunction with a local furnishing store
- Designing, specifying and supervising interior renovation of two Grade II listed properties in heritage area
- Bringing the project in on budget and contributing to a £100k profit for the developer

Career History:

1990 to Present: Self-Employed
Designer and decorator
Designed domestic and retail interiors:
- Assessed client requirements
- Negotiated fees and budget with client
- Selected suitable wall coverings, furnishings and fabrics
- Presented proposals to clients
- Bought from UK and overseas sources
- Created specialist decorative paint finishes
- Liaised between client and sub-contractors
- Worked to pre-agreed time scale and budget

1985–1990: Marc D'Araby Furniture Galleries Ltd
Display Designer
Designed showroom and point-of-sale displays for retail chain throughout the South of England:

- Assessed requirements of individual store managers
- Designed 'customer-friendly' display settings
- Drew up fully detailed plans and instructions for installation by local contractors
- Supervised final stages and set dressing
- Maintained, renovated and updated displays

1981–1985: Sollways of Liverpool
Display Designer
Window Dresser
Undertook window dressing, in-store display and promotion of home and garden products as part of display team for large city-centre department store.
Promoted to Display Designer in 1983.

1980–1981: The Curtain House
Window Dresser
Sales Assistant
Advised clients on suitability and quantities for curtaining and soft furnishings. Designed, executed and maintained window displays.

Education and Training:
1978–1980: City College
Retail Display Certificate Course
    Marketing and Retailing
    Retail and Retail Display
    Point of Sale Merchandising
    Advertising and Promotion

1973–1978: East Faringdean School
    Five 'O' levels, including Maths and English

Personal Details:
Date of birth: 8 June 1962
Interests: Member of the South of England Water-colour Society and the Women Mean Business Club. Enjoys dancing and antique collecting

Car owner/driver with full, clean, UK licence

References available on request

Alan Moorhouse

23 The Avenue
Seaton Parva
Hampshire HA3 6TL

Tel. 0000 0000000

Career Profile:

A writer and broadcaster with a total of 15 years' experience including seven years as a regular contributor to Radio Hampshire. An effective communicator with a track record of successful books, articles and radio pieces on local history and regional issues, based on a thorough understanding of journalism.

Key Experience:

Writing

- Researching and writing *Buckler's Hard* – the story of Henry Adams, Nelson's ship-builder
- Compiling three local guide books:
  - Romsey Rambles
  - Winchester Wanders
  - Portsmouth Parade
- Editing Tourist Board publications:
  - *Days Out On the South Coast – Portsmouth and District*
  - *Days Out On the South Coast – The New Forest*
- Writing a regular 'Local Heroes' column for *Portsmouth Pickings*
- Contributing over 100 articles on local history and natural history for the *South Hampshire Chronicle* and *Points Around* magazine

Broadcasting

- Dramatising *Buckler's Hard* for Radio Hampshire
- Broadcasting regular 10- and 20-minute reports on items of local interest on 'Out and About'
- Writing and presenting 30-minute promotional video for South-crest Hotels, 'Blow The Man Down'

Career History:

1992 to Present
Freelance Writer
Clients include:

- Hampshire Press Ltd
- Tourist Information Board
- Tourist Services Ltd
- Portsmouth Gazette Publications

- Southcrest Holdings Ltd
- Radio Hampshire
- Daniel Deckland and Co. Ltd

1989 to 1992
South Downs Heritage Centre
Publications Manager
Compiled, catalogued and promoted publications of interest to visitors to the Heritage Centre, and for use as a local information resource.

1980 to 1989
South Hampshire Chronicle
Features Editor
Reporter
Edited newspaper articles on local events. Researched and wrote regular column. Reported on local issues. Promoted to Features Editor in 1985.

Education and Training:

1978–1980 College of Trade and Commerce
Diploma in Journalism

1974–1977 South Eastern University
BA History and English

1967–1974 Oversands High School
'A' levels: English History French
'O' levels: eight, including English and Maths

Personal Details:

Date of birth:	17 August 1956
Interests:	Natural History
	Member of South Down Botanical Society
	Member of the Tallinger local history group
	Voluntary tutor on the local literacy initiative scheme

Car owner/driver with full, clean, UK licence

References available on request

Hannah Gansa
Flat 4 Tily Court Mansions
London
SW9 0PP

Tel. 0000 000000

CAREER OBJECTIVE
An experienced assistant editor and photographer with a background in specialist craft books and magazines. Possessing well-developed communication and inter-personal skills along with a high degree of technical competence and a commitment to quality, I am now looking for a challenging position where these characteristics and achievements can be used to maximum effect.

KEY EXPERIENCE AND ACHIEVEMENTS
- Planning and implementing visual policy for two leading magazines in their field
- Developing key areas within the subject field
- Winning 'Craft Magazine of the Year' two years in succession
- Successfully implementing editorial policy
- Liaising tactfully with authors and freelance contributors
- Designing and co-writing promotional material
- Coordinating public relations, publicity and press releases

CAREER HISTORY
Fairport Magazines Ltd
Needles and Threads
Happy Hands
1992 to Present
Assistant Editor/Photographer
Designed and organised photographs and photographic policy for the magazines:
- Designed, set up and photographed photographic spreads
- Organised and photographed 'step-by-step' instruction series in conjunction with crafts-people
- Edited freelance submissions to journal standard
- Researched and developed new fields of interest to readership
- Solicited contributions from craft-workers
- Covered exhibitions and conventions for news items, ideas and information
- Organised and carried out interviews and photographic sessions with subjects

Cotswolds Crafts Publications Ltd
1988 to 1992
Editorial Assistant
Prepared written material for publication:
- Reviewed copy for errors in spelling, syntax and punctuation
- Ensured manuscripts conformed to house style and editorial policy
- Conferred with authors regarding copy changes
- Marked copy for typesetting using standard symbols
- Selected and prepared photographs and illustrations

Berholt Freeman Ltd
1985 to 1988
Marketing Assistant
Assisted with company marketing and promotion:
- Produced annual report, press releases, newsletter, and brochures
- Liaised with ad. agencies, printers, art directors, audio-visual and video producers
- Coordinated public relations exercises
- Organised inclusion in exhibitions and trade shows

Dollar Holdings
1983 to 1985
Secretary to Marketing Department
- Provided secretarial cover for the department
- Assisted marketing personnel where appropriate

EDUCATION AND TRAINING
Three Acres College of Art and Technology
1990 to 1992 (part-time)
Certificate of Photographic Studies

Sperring Sixth Form College/CFE
1981 to 1983
RSA II Secretarial Certificate
GCE 'A' levels – English, Art, French

Turnall Secondary School
1976 to 1981
GCE 'O' levels – six including English and Maths

PERSONAL
Date of birth:	1 May 1965
Health:	Non-smoker
Licence:	Full, clean, UK driver's licence
Interests:	Member of local amateur orchestra
	Music appreciation
	Swimming
	Aromatherapy
References:	Available on request

LUKE JUMP

56 Ballard Place
Ashworthy
Oxfordshire OX14 5LA

Home: 0000 0000000
Work: 0000 0000000

Career Profile

A high level of professionalism offered by an experienced graphic artist in return for challenge, job satisfaction and the opportunity to build on existing experience. With the proven ability to understand client requirements and deliver effective creative solutions within specified deadlines, the ability to use modern technology in the production of graphic material complements a wide range of traditional skills, along with well-developed communication skills honed by extensive dealings with senior management and other professionals.

Key Experience

- Working with Macintosh graphics packages:
  - Xpress
  - Illustrator
  - Photoshop
- Working with four-colour reproduction
- Liaising, consulting and negotiating with clients, including:
  - Hallen & Shore
  - LLK
  - Employment Services Commission
  - Playnet Computers
  - Kase UK
- Art director of agency winning 'Media Standard' award 1995 and 1996

Career History

Brand Response

1994–Present

Art Director

Devised concepts and supervised staff in preparing layout designs for artwork and copy for direct marketing agency:

- Consulted with client companies with regard to aims and objectives, presentation and budget
- Formulated layout and design concept
- Produced, selected or arranged to have produced suitable material for artwork and/or illustrations
- Supervised staff preparing layouts for printing
- Approved final layout for presentation to client

116

Wells Strata Deanery
1992–1994
Assistant Studio Manager
Assisted organisation and running of studio together with production of high-grade computer graphics for audio-visual company:
- Created a range of graphics for flipcharts, OHP, 35mm, video presentations and slide animations
- Supervised allocation of projects
- Briefed and monitored freelance staff

News Review Publications Ltd
1990–1992
Designer
Produced graphic material for company bulletins, brochures, annual reports and in-house magazines

PAC Magazines Ltd
1989–1990
Paste-up Artist
Produced paste-ups and mechanicals for magazines

Education and Training
Work-related training:
Quark Xpress
Photoshop
Illustrator

South Counties College of Art and Design
1985 to 1988
Diploma in Art and Design

John Galliard School
1978 to 1985
'A' levels – English, Art
'O' levels – six, including English and Technical Drawing

Personal Details
Date of birth: 16 September 1967

Licence: Full, clean, UK driving licence

Interests: Marathon running
Swimming
Hill walking and climbing

References: Available on request

Barbra Kingdom

41A Pine Court Gardens
Landschurch Down
Avon AV5 1MR

Tel. 0000 0000000

Career Profile:

An innovative and intelligent video maker, with first-rate experience gained designing and producing videos for a broad range of clients. Adept at working with a wide variety of people effectively and good-humouredly in sometimes highly demanding situations. Skilled at evaluating and resolving problems creatively

Key Experience:

- Video and Film
  - Planning, producing and directing seven 30–60 minute videos for The Parenting Initiative, including 'Introducing Baby Massage', 'Baby Talk', 'Little White Lies' and 'What Does It Mean When . . .?'
  - Deciding with featured expert the content and presentation of the topic on video
  - Planning lighting, camera angles, camera shots
  - Assisting youth group making youth and community videos
  - Training them in use of video equipment and basics of production and editing
  - Designing, producing and directing two independent video shorts – 'Moon Viewing Platform', and 'All Things Bright And Beautiful' shown at the Arts South West Film Festival
- Editing
  - Machine-to-machine video editing
  - Coordinating sound, content and storyline
  - Dubbing
  - Super 8 film viewing, editing and splicing
- Radio
  - Researching, planning and presenting weekly community arts slot on local radio
  - Delivering reports
  - Selecting, approaching and interviewing guests

Career History:
1990 to Present
Video Maker
Community Production Facility

Radio Producer and Presenter
Valley Radio

Video Trainer/Facilitator
Kids TV
Community Youth Group

Education and Training:
1986–1990 Wessex College of Art and Technology
BTEC HND Media and Visual Studies

Vocational Studies:
       The Moving Image
       Twentieth Century Film
       The National Film Archive

1979–1986 East Faringdean School
       'O' levels – five, including English Language
       'A' levels – English and Art

Personal Details:
Date of birth: 15 September 1968

Interests: Film, Video and Music

Car owner/driver with full, clean, UK licence

References available on request

11

CVs for Clerical and Administrative Jobs

Clerks and administrators ensure that an organisation runs smoothly and efficiently. It's important that a prospective employer reading your CV believes that you will, first and foremost, take over the vacancy smoothly, effectively and as proficiently as possible, with very little disruption to the department. The most important areas to emphasise, therefore, are your current skills and past experience as these will be the best guide to your future performance.

The key qualities employers usually look for in applicants for clerical and administrative jobs are:

- Organisation
- Dependability
- A methodical approach
- The ability to work with others
- Specific technical skills
- Experience in specific areas.

What are the main points, then, for a clerical and administrative CV?

KEY SKILLS

Many clerical, administrative and secretarial jobs call for specific skills such as word-processing or bookkeeping skills, use of a particular sort of switchboard, use of particular computer software packages, or knowledge of a specific language.

Include all your relevant skills, and highlight the specific skills required for the position in your Key Skills section so that they can be clearly seen.

KEY EXPERIENCE

Experience in a specific field is often a job requirement – a computer services administrator will have a different area of knowledge and expertise from a personnel administrator. Include experience such as supervision and planning that will be relevant to most positions, then choose key experience – payroll procedures, customer services, whatever – to fit the job you are applying for.

CAREER HISTORY

Concentrate on areas of responsibility, skills used and experience gained. Include improvements in departmental efficiency you have introduced.

Some people find that their clerical or administrative jobs have been essentially similar in content. In this case concentrate on emphasising Key Skills and Key Experience and simply summarise your actual Career History.

The examples on the following pages show an outline CV which includes both a Key Skills and a Key Experience section, and CVs which make use of some or all of these points:

1. **Outline CV**
2. **Amanda Barwell** – Clerical assistant
3. **Tessa Dixon** – Secretary
4. **Valerie Andrews** – Secretarial and financial administrator
5. **Philip McVickery** – Information Technology Administrator
6. **Rose Mary Tan** – Records administrator.

(**Your Name** in large, bold type)
(Your full address)

(Postcode)

(Telephone number, including area code)

Personal Profile

(A brief, business-like description of yourself)

(Personal qualities)

(Experience)

(Skills and personal strengths)

Key Skills

- (The main skills you have developed)
- (Particularly those appropriate to the job you are applying for)
-
-
-

Key Experience

- (Your main areas of experience)
- (Particularly those appropriate to the job you are applying for)
-
-

Career History

(**Name of Company**, usually starting with the most recent)

(Dates you worked there)

(Job title)

(Brief description of what you did)

(Brief description of what you achieved in this position)

-
-
-

(**Name of Company**)

(Dates you worked there)

(Job title)

(Brief description of what you did)

(Brief description of what you achieved in this position)

-
-
-

(Name of Company)

(Dates you worked there)

(Job title)

(Brief description of what you did. Jobs you did some years ago require less detail than your more recent ones)

Education and Training

(Starting with the highest, most recent OR most relevant qualification)

(Name of school, college, or university)

(Dates you attended)

(The qualification you achieved)

(You could include brief details of what was covered in the course, especially if recently qualified)

-
-
-
-
-

(Name of school, college, or university)

(Dates you attended)

(The qualification you achieved)

(Name of school, college, or university)

(Dates you attended)

(The qualification you achieved)

(Don't go back further than your senior or secondary school)

(Professional Training)

(Details of any professional training undertaken at work)

- (Qualification or skill achieved)
-
-
-
-

Personal Details

(Date of birth)

(Driving licence)

(Married or single – only if relevant)

(Nationality – only if relevant)

(Interests and activities. Brief details)

(References – usually 'available on request')

Amanda Barwell

5 Juniper Court
Nine Trees
Devon DV22 1JC

Tel. 0000 0000000

Personal Profile:

A competent and efficient clerical assistant with experience of accounts, order office and general office work. Punctual, reliable and methodical, good at handling a variety of tasks efficiently, with a strong aptitude for organisation and administration.

Key Skills:

- Keyboard skills - 40 wpm
- Operating
  - fax machine
  - photocopiers - Canon and Rank Xerox
  - franking machine
- Preparing and writing routine correspondence
- Organising and carrying out routine administrative work
  - maintaining records
  - dealing with incoming telephone calls
  - dealing with incoming mail

Key Experience:

- Clerk-typist
  - typing from manuscript
  - completing and despatching reports
  - maintaining files
  - organising appointments
  - cover for reception and switchboard
- Order clerk
  - processing orders
  - raising order codes
  - preparing dockets and despatching emergency orders
  - filing and retrieving despatch notes, orders and delivery records
- Accounts clerk
  - documenting accounts
  - preparing correspondence
  - processing invoices, cheques, credit and debit notes, payments and receipts
  - inputting data on to computer files

Career History:

Kellington Park College
1993 to Present
Clerk Typist

West End Office Contracts Ltd
1990 to 1993
Clerical Assistant

Dobson Dean & Co Ltd
1988 to 1990
Clerk Typist

Hindway Ltd
1987 to 1988
Clerical Assistant

Southcross Hospital
1984 to 1987
Clerical Assistant

Education:

East Devon Open Learning Centre
1995
- Introduction to Computer Literacy
- Pitman Intermediate Office Practice

Whitcombe College
1983 to 1984
- RSA Stage I Keyboard Skills
- RSA Stage I Office Skills
- Pitman Elementary Office Practice

Marsh Cross School
- 1978–1983
- Seven 'O' levels including Maths, English and Commerce

Personal Details:

Date of birth: 19 January 1967
Interests: Aerobics, swimming and walking
Full, clean, UK driving licence
References available on request

TESSA DIXON
61 Chantry Hill
Stoke Dean, Essex EX3 5DM

Tel: 0000 0000000

Personal Profile

A highly trained and experienced personal secretary with excellent shorthand and word-processing skills, who has developed, as secretary to the managing director of a prominent property company, first-rate organisational skills and initiative. A loyal, supportive professional, used to prioritising a demanding workload under pressure.

Key Skills

Secretarial skills
- Pitman Private Secretary Diploma
- Keyboard - 70 wpm
- Shorthand - 120 wpm
- Audio typing
- Commercial correspondence

Computer Skills
- Word Perfect 5.1
- Word 6.0 and Word 6.0 for Windows
- Ami Pro 5.0
- Display Write 4
- Lotus 123

Other skills
- Electronic mail system
- Telecom Gold
- Financial software
- Graphic software

Experience

- Ten years' secretarial experience in a wide range of environments
- Three years' experience as Confidential Secretary to Managing Director
- An understanding of business and the secretary's role therein
- A clear commitment to efficiency
- Knowledge of good office practice and procedures
- An established track record in effective office support

Career Summary

Heath McIllany Properties
1992 to Present
Confidential Secretary
Provided full secretarial support:
- Typed letters, memoranda and reports with due regard to confidentiality
- Compiled monthly reports and statistics
- Organised meetings, took and typed minutes
- Arranged accommodation and travel for staff and overseas visitors
- Coordinated diary and appointments for MD
- Communicated with overseas clients

Dockland Industrial Company
1990 to 1992
Personal Secretary
Provided secretarial support to head of section:
- Arranged internal and external meetings
- Took minutes at meetings and typed them up along with summaries and reports for other departments
- Organised all resulting correspondence and enquiries
- Liaised with outside agencies in the production of reports

Timberland Insurance
1988 to 1990
Department Secretary
Provided secretarial support for New Business Team

Stanegate Holdings Ltd
1985 to 1988
Personal Secretary
Shorthand Typist

Education and Training

Member of the Institute of Qualified Private Secretaries

1991–1992 City Adult Education College (Part-time/evening course)
- Pitman Private Secretary Diploma
- Pitman Commercial Correspondence
- Pitman Shorthand

1983–1985 Westmordale College of Education
- RSA III Typewriting (Distinction)
- RSA III Shorthand and Typewriting Certificate
- RSA III Audio-typing
- RSA II English Language

1977–1982 Clevedon School
'O' levels:
Five including Maths and English

Personal Details

Date of birth:	9 October 1966
Health:	Non-smoker
Licence:	Full, clean, UK driver's licence
Interests:	Theatre and cinema
References:	Available on request

Valerie Andrews
43 Newton Street,
Northampton N14 5ET

Tel: 0000 0000000

Personal Profile
A well-organised, reliable administrative assistant and secretary with extensive knowledge of good office practice, and a wealth of experience in both large and small companies. Hardworking and trustworthy, with the ability to remain good humoured and unflappable under pressure.

Key Qualifications

- RSA III Typewriting – current speed 70 wpm
- RSA II Audio-typing – current speed 70 wpm
- RSA II Shorthand – current speed 120 wpm
- RSA II Secretarial Studies
- City & Guilds CLAIT

Key Experience

Secretarial
- Confidential Secretary to Personnel Director
- Secretary to Finance Manager
- Secretary to Marketing Department
- Typing reports and correspondence
- Setting up agendas and minuting all departmental meetings
- Organising client presentations and corporate entertainment

Administrative
- Responsible for day-to-day running of ten-person department
- Answerable for all secretarial staff administration
- Coordinating department work schedules
- Training and supervising junior staff

Financial Administration
- Compiling monthly budget reports
- Preparing quantity audits, projections, and financial statements
- Responsible for raising orders and invoicing for office stationery and consumables
- Supervising accounts payable and accounts receivable

Career Summary
Heathfield Enterprises Ltd, Northampton
1992 to Present
Office Manager

Somerhill & Hayes Ltd, Ipswich
1988 to 1992
Administrative Assistant
Personal Secretary

International Supplies Ltd, Ipswich
1986 to 1988
Personal Secretary

Donald F Martin & Co. Ltd, Preston
1983 to 1986
Department Secretary

Tanstead Personnel Ltd, Preston
1980 to 1983
Temporary Secretarial/ Clerical positions

Education and Training
1977–1979 North Preston College of Education
RSA Secretarial Certificate
RSA Stage II
RSA Stage III

1970–1977 Clevedon School
'O' levels:
Five including Maths and English
'A' levels:
English, French and Commerce

Personal Details
Date of birth: 21 April 1959

Health: Non-smoker

Interests: Badminton, swimming.
Member of the local Operatic Society

References: Available on request

Philip McVickery
66 Cleve Way
St Aldans
Hollingtree
Leicestershire LE17 8UK

Tel. 0000 0000000

Personal Profile
A computer-literate administrator with a sound background in the use of information technology in the workplace. Accurate, persistent and self-reliant, with the ability to pick up ideas quickly and approach problems logically. Experience of working with the public has taught the value of tact and diplomacy as well as a degree of assertiveness. Calm under pressure and with the proven ability to be reliable in a crisis.

Key Qualifications
- Finance for Administrators
  — Budgeting for contract tenders for government funding
  — Budgeting to precise figures
- Computer skills:
  — JSP structured programme design
  — VAX 780 computer system
  — Excel and SuperCalc spreadsheet applications
  — Access database
  — Word 6.0 and Wordperfect 5.1 word-processing

Key Skills
- Understanding and using information technology
- Interpreting instructions and carrying out policies accurately
- Dealing with people effectively, tactfully and efficiently
- Analysing problems and providing solutions
- Planning work to meet deadlines

Career History
Keyline Youth Trust
1992–Present
Administrator
Ran administrative department on a day-to-day basis, including:
- Budget control and petty cash
- Premises management
- Designed and implemented administrative procedures in office
- Traced and acted upon all outstanding bills and invoices
- Rationalised entry of information on to database with the result that the Trust's business was more accurately represented

JJ Hey Ltd
1987–1992
System Controller
Ran computer system for six offices, including:
- Routine hardware maintenance
- Data back-up
- Provided help-desk facility
- Facilitated effective staff usage of all computer facilities
- Monitored printing and stationery costs and implemented cost-effective measures

Lake & Stewart Insurance Ltd
1982–1987
Claims Supervisor
Assessed claims for redundancy insurance, including:
- Assessed claims
- Maintained cheque issue deadlines
- Supervised up to seven staff members
- Maintained and administered insurance certificate stocks
- Revised wording of unemployment benefit monthly claim forms resulting in 12% reduction in errors
- Established criteria for conversion of clerical claims to computer operation resulting in minimal disruption for clients

Department of Employment
1976–1980
Clerical Officer
Processed claims for unemployment benefit

Education and Training

1971–1975 Chesterfield College of Education
Certificate of Education
Education Theory, English and Drama

1988–1993 Tembury South School
'O' levels:
Five including Maths and English
'A' levels:
English and Art

Personal Details

Date of birth: 9 February 1953

References: Available on request

Rose Mary Tan
4A Sandle Lane
Churchdean
Dorset
DR12 3BL

Tel. 0000 0000000

Career Profile
A thorough and methodical records administrator, with extensive experience in the verification, storage and retrieval of records both as documents and on computer databases.

Key Qualifications

- Database and record systems
  — Access database
  — D-base 3
  — MediWatch tailored statistical package
- Computer skills:
  — Excel
  — SuperCalc
  — Word For Windows 6.0
  — Wordperfect 5.1

Key Skills

- Maintaining, developing and administering medical records and data systems
- Supervising staff compiling and inputting record data, and storing documents
- Collecting, storing and retrieving patient data
- Formulating strategies for handling high volume records
- Implementing effective procedures for storage and retrieval
- Developing 'user-friendly' methods for staff processing
- Undertaking first-stage statistical analysis
- Preparing and supplying information for staff and departments

Career History
Porterhouse Hospital Trust
1990–Present
Records Administrator
Experienced in all aspects of receiving, storing, retrieving and supplying data:
- Supervised up to ten staff
- Maintained and updated records and files
- Checked records in and out

- Noted inconsistencies and queried as necessary
- Processed both documents and computerised records and print-outs

Fordice Road Health Centre
1986–1990
Administrative Assistant
Provided clerical and administrative support to Centre Administrator:
- Maintained and updated records
- Input and retrieved data and statistical information
- Coordinated communication between staff, clinics and clinic users
- Monitored usage of consumables

Department of Employment
1984–1986
Clerical Officer
Clerical Worker
- Processed claims for unemployment benefit
- Maintained and updated client records

Education and Training

Blare Petrie College
- Introduction to Computer Literacy
- Working with Spreadsheets
- Working with Databases:
  — introductory to advanced level
  — working with windows databases

Torburymouth Senior School
'O' levels:
Five including Maths and English

Personal Details

Date of birth: 30 March 1968

Interests: Opera and classical ballet
                    Gardening

References: Available on request

12

CVs for Sales and Marketing Jobs

Sales people ensure that a company sells its products and makes a profit. A prospective employer reading your CV is looking for confirmation that you will be able to sell their goods or services and increase profits for them. The most important thing to emphasise, therefore, is your past success in doing this.

The key qualities employers usually look for in applicants for sales jobs are:

- The ability to sell
- Tenacity and perseverance
- Competence
- The ability to get on with others
- Energy, commitment and enthusiasm.

What will help you get these points across?

CAREER PROFILE

An idea of the areas you have covered in the past, the sort of experience you have had to date, and your current position in your career, will all be helpful information to a potential employer.

If you have experience outside of sales but relevant to the job you are applying for, include it. Buyers like to feel they are dealing with someone who understands what they're talking about.

KEY ACHIEVEMENTS

Companies want sales people who can work hard and make money. Let them know what you're capable of doing. If you regularly exceed targets, have a habit of increasing profits or always get the most orders, make sure they know about it.

CAREER HISTORY

This is where you can put actual facts and figures to the claims you have made about your achievements. Outline your performance with past companies and expand on your successes, rather than just stating your responsibilities.

The examples on the following pages show an outline CV including a Key Achievement section, and CVs which make use of some or all of the above points:

1. **Outline CV**
2. **Linda Knauf** – Telesales
3. **Paul A Hendry** – Retail store manager
4. **Paige McLeod** – Salesperson and sales manager
5. **Francis Scott** – Sales/product manager
6. **Ruth Sefton** – Media executive.

(Your Name in large, bold type)
(Your full address)

_____

_____

_____

(Postcode)

(Telephone number, including area code)

Career Profile

(A brief, business-like description of yourself)

(Skills)

(Experience)

(Personal strengths)

Key Achievements

- (The main things you have achieved)
- (Particularly those appropriate to the job you are applying for)
-
-
-

Career History

(Name of Company, usually starting with the most recent)

(Dates you worked there)

(Job title)

(Brief description of what you did)

(Brief description of what you achieved in this position)

-
-
-

(Name of Company)

(Dates you worked there)

(Job title)

(Brief description of what you did)

(Brief description of what you achieved in this position)

-
-
-

(Name of Company)

(Dates you worked there)

(Job title)

(Brief description of what you did. Jobs you did some years ago require less detail than your more recent ones)

Education and Training

(Starting with the highest, most recent OR most relevant qualification)

(Name of school, college, or university)

(Dates you attended)

(The qualification you achieved)

(You could include brief details of what was covered in the course, especially if recently qualified)

-
-
-
-
-

(Name of school, college, or university)

(Dates you attended)

(The qualification you achieved)

(Name of school, college, or university)

(Dates you attended)

(The qualification you achieved)

(Don't go back further than your senior or secondary school)

(Professional Training)

(Details of any professional training undertaken at work)

- (Qualification or skill achieved)
-
-
-

Personal Details

(Date of birth)

(Driving licence)

(Married or single – only if relevant)

(Nationality – only if relevant)

(Interests and activities. Brief details)

(References – usually 'available on request')

Linda Knauf

Flat 4
115 Trebarton Road
Colby
Bucks BK11 7CW

Tel. 0000 0000000

Personal Profile:

A trained and positive telesales professional with experience in financial sales, communications and specialist publishing, and a background in customer services. Ready, willing and able to play a key role in company development.

Key Achievements:

- Consistently meeting and exceeding targets by 10–15%
- Achieving 110% increase in sales for new territory
- Winning 'top team' award for home improvement sales
- Successfully combining customer care service with new business development programme
- Achieving NVQ 2 in Telephone Selling:
  - Gaining customer attention and interest
  - Projecting company image effectively
  - Winning appointments
  - Handling objections positively and professionally

Career History:

Auto Credit Europe plc
1994 to Present
Telesales/Aftercare service
- Advised customers how to finance their car purchase
- Negotiated with all types of customers
- Worked effectively with field sales team
- Achieved weekly average sales of £25K worth of cover
- Optimised profit opportunities and sales performance, contributing to an overall centre sales increase of 10%
- Increased sales of financial packages and add-on products by 17%

Redhouse Publications
1992 to 1994
Advertisement sales
- Successfully sold advertising space for two best-selling computer magazines
- Operated in a highly competitive environment
- Achieved 15% increase in sales over and above target

Laurell Communications Ltd
1990 to 1992
Telesales
- Effectively sold mobile communications systems to businesses
- Assisted in building up new territory in South Midlands
- Achieved 110% new business growth in first year, 40% ahead of target

Wallmix Ltd
1989 to 1990
Telesales
- Cold called to arranged appointments for sales team
- Consistently exceeded target calls by 15%
- Consistently exceeded appointments target by 10%

D'Arblay Connaught
1987 to 1989
Customer Service Advisor

Terrence Farrow & Partners
1984 to 1987
Clerical Assistant

Education:
Auto Credit Europe Training Centre
- NVQ Telephone Selling level 1
- NVQ Telephone Selling level 2

Bistock Secretarial College
1983 to 1984
- RSA Stage I Keyboard Skills
- RSA Stage I Office Skills

South West District School
- 1976–1983
- Five 'O' levels including Maths, English and French
- Two 'A' levels – French and English

Personal Details:
Date of birth: 3 May 1965
Health: Non-smoker
Interests: Team sports – Netball
Women's League American Football
Volleyball

Full, clean, UK driving licence
References available on request

Paul A Hendry

6 Yellow Stone Crescent
Headford
Staffordshire
ST15 6YY

Tel. 0000 0000000

Career Profile:

An experienced store manager with a solid background in high turnover supermarket environments in a wide variety of locations.

Key Skills:

- Increasing sales turnover
- Improving customer service and satisfaction
- Motivating staff
- Maintaining tight control of stock
- Working as part of a team
- Working efficiently at speed and under pressure
- Communicating effectively at all levels

Career Achievements:

Starfrost Frozen Foods Ltd
Various locations – four stores in all
1990 to Present
Store Manager

- Increased turnover by around £10k in each of three different stores during time as manager
- Regularly achieved turnover of £25k–£40k depending on store location
- Achieved a record-breaking Xmas turnover of £126k
- Maintained year-on-year increases of 10–15%
- Maintained level of turnover in Bath store despite extensive refurbishment
- Obtained wines and beers licence for two stores
- Improved stock control and shrinkage
- Supervised staff retraining

Freezer-Foods Ltd
Various locations – ten stores in all
1983 to 1990
Store Manager

- Increased turnover of Teddington store from £18k to £25k
- Increased turnover from £27k to £35k in Edgware store
- Increased annual turnover by an average of 15–20%
- Ensured each store was promoted to a higher division during time as manager
- Successfully handled two cases of gross misconduct
- Promoted from Assistant Manager in 1985

HMS Hollens
1982 to 1983
Manager
Bar manager on Royal Navy Base, responsible for the day-to-day running of the bar; organised staff, entertainment and administration.

Shield Market Ltd
1978 to 1982
Grocery Manager
Organised daily running of the department including hiring staff, ordering stock, and achieving set targets. Promoted from Assistant Manager.

Hereford Stores Ltd
1974 to 1978
Assistant Grocery Manager
Organised daily running of grocery department including administration, staff training, and customer service.

Various
1972 to 1974
Sales assistant and warehouse assistant – various positions.

Work Related Training:

Starfrost Frozen Foods Ltd:
    EPOS; FAST; OS2; STOP; SAS
Freezer-Foods Ltd Training Centre:
    Customer Care Awareness Course (Certificate)
    Basic Management Techniques
    Business Systems IBM Computer Course
    Instore Management EPOS Computer Course
ShieldCo Training Centre:
    Merchandising to Increase sales
    Security Awareness
    Stock and Ordering
    Administration
    Achieving Monthly Targets
    Health and Safety
    Staff Training, Appraisals and Motivation
    Staff Management Techniques

Personal Details:

Date of birth:	21 June 1956
Interests:	Squash – local league player; cycling; skiing; watersports Foreign travel and cookery
Licence:	Full, clean, UK licence
References:	Available on request

PAIGE MCLEOD
Flat 2
18 Brinsley Square
London SE17 7FS

Tel: 0000 0000000

Career Profile

A highly trained salesperson experienced in business-to-business sales and sales management, with a clear understanding of company structures and the decision-making process. A successful, profit-driven individual with a proven record of achievement, capable of making a significant contribution to the profitability of any employer.

Key Achievements

- Achieving 120% increase in uptake of technical support services
- Increasing sales by up to 15% annually
- Directing highly successful sales team to top company awards
- Winning Top Salesperson Award
- Achieving:
  — Diploma in Marketing
  — Certified Diploma in Accounting and Finance
  — Diploma in Management Studies

Career Summary

Mildenhall Business Systems
1990 to Present
Regional Manager
Responsible for seven retail centres.
- Targeted technical support services and increased uptake by 120%
- Consistently exceeded targets
- Raised profile and increased enquiries by 25%
- Increased sales by 15%
- Improved profits by 12% overall
- Monitored sales statistics and controlled stock levels and ordering
- Assessed and trained sales staff

The Business Business
1986 to 1990
Sales Manager
Responsible for own territory plus sales team of five people:
- Increased overall profits by 7–15%
- Consistently met and exceeded personal sales targets
- Set team sales budgets, assigned territories and targets
- Undertook staff reviews and training

Direction Office Machines
1981 to 1986
Sales Executive
- Developed virgin territory
- Exceeded target performance by 5%
- Planned marketing campaigns for sales promotion
- Achieved 55% increase in enquiries at peak of promotion

Brook Copiers Ltd
1979 to 1981
Sales Executive
- Exceeded all area sales targets
- Achieved Top Twenty National Sales Award

Various
1975 to 1979
Retail Sales
Telesales

Education and Training

Member of the Professional Sales and Marketing Society

Institute of Business, Sales and Marketing
- 1991 – Diploma in Management Studies
- 1987 – Diploma in Marketing

Highbank College
- 1980 – Certified Diploma in Accounting and Finance

Pinder Dobson School
'O' levels:
Five including Maths and English

Personal Details

Date of birth:	17 October 1959
Health:	Non-smoker
Licence:	Full, clean, UK driver's licence
Interests:	Theatre and cinema
References:	Available on request

Francis Scott
12 Nuffield Crescent
Bowerby
Sunderland SN6 7ZP

Tel. 0000 0000000

Career Profile:
A personable, confident and enthusiastic professional with solid experience in sales, marketing and management, and a history of successful career moves in both voluntary organisations and the private sector. Adept at mixing dynamism with the ability to assimilate information at all levels and using this information to achieve the desired results

Key Skills:
- Managing accounts and maintaining long-term customer relationships
- Motivating, developing and recruiting staff, including staff training and incentives
- Planning and controlling sales resources to maximum effect
- Maintaining cash flow and profitability
- Analysing and evaluating sales results
- Planning and implementing public relations and advertising campaigns

Career Achievements:
The Wellness Initiative
1995 to Present
Area Manager
Managed North East region of national medical charity:

- Worked towards Institute of Management NVQ level 4
- Took over and re-established area that had fallen into neglect
- Built up team of trained, professional volunteers
- Established efficient collection service
- Produced and implemented marketing plan
- Improved methods of forwarding donations

Dakk & Taylor Ltd
1992 to 1995
Sales/Product Manager

- Organised and established new product range from concept to completion
- Took over two neglected product ranges and revitalised them
- Organised continuous training programme for internal and external sales personnel with training in sales and product knowledge
- Planned and organised exhibitions and seminars
- Prepared and delivered presentations at all levels including hands-on product demonstrations to groups of all sizes
- Directly responsible to the Managing Director and Sales and Marketing Director for all aspects relating to the promotion and sale of product range

Sensor (UK) Ltd
1987 to 1992
Product Manager
- Successfully increased sales year-on-year
- Maintained profitability of product range
- Organised consistently innovative public relations and advertising campaign
- Introduced and marketed new product ranges
- Trained and managed sales team
- Supervised customer orders and oversaw stock control

Avonside Ltd
1983 to 1987
Sales Manager
- Increased sales turnover
- Introduced new products and marketing ideas
- Recruited and trained sales team

FFG Co
1978 to 1983
Key Account Manager
Sales Representative
- Proved ability as sales representative and promoted to Key Accounts Manager in 1980

Education:

Institute of Management
- NVQ Sales and Marketing Management level 4

Terrence Keeler Secondary School
1970 to 1977
- 'A' level: Mathematics
- 'O' level: seven including Maths and English

Personal Details:

Date of birth: 11 March 1959
Health: Non-smoker
Interests: Badminton
                Riding
                Computing

Full, clean, UK driving licence
References available on request

Ruth Sefton
78 Eastway Road
East Reach
Essex
EX11 9AK

Tel. 0000 0000000

Career Profile
An innovative and intelligent media executive, with extensive experience of both planning and buying in all media.

Key Achievement
- Conceiving, planning and implementing innovative media buying to tremendous effect in Maxtape 'Name That Tune' campaign, involving:
  — Analysing target market
  — Discovering life-style trend favouring use of low-cost early-morning television slots
  — Obtaining maximum exposure to target audience for minimal budget
  — Campaign won Miller Silver Award

Career History
The Advertising People
1989–Present
Media Executive
Assistant Media Planner
Recommended appropriate and effective media for agency clients:

- Participated in preliminary talks with clients alongside Account Executive
- Analysed target market and marketing objectives
- Formulated media strategy
- Prepared detailed media plans
- Negotiated media rates
- Responsible for £2.5 million multimedia television account, and £1.75 million print media account
- Supervised current assistant planner
- Promoted from Assistant Media Planner to Media Executive in 1992

Range, Klein and Morrisey
1986–1989
Media Buyer
- Analysed data from NRS and BARB
- Prepared media strategy for direct marketing clients
- Negotiated with media representatives for best rates
- Kept detailed records of all transactions

The Word Factory
1984–1986
Personal Assistant
- Provided administrative support to Media Director and Media Department

Education and Training

North Western University
BA English Literature (2.2)

Edward Marshall School
'O' levels: seven including Maths and English
'A' levels: English, French and History

Personal Details

Date of birth: 21 June 1963

Interests: Modern dance
Fine art and antiques
Travel

Licence: Full, clean, UK driving licence

References: Available on request

13

CVs for Technical Jobs

Technical personnel are required to carry out processes or production methods smoothly, accurately and efficiently.

It's important that a prospective employer reading your CV believes that you have the technical expertise – the knowledge and experience – to take over the vacancy efficiently, with as little disruption to the department as possible. The most important areas to emphasise, therefore, are your technical competence, experience, and qualifications and training as these will be the best guide to your likely performance.

The key qualities employers usually look for in applicants for technical jobs are:

- Specific technical skills
- Experience in specific areas
- Dependability and accuracy
- A methodical approach
- Organisation
- The ability to work with others.

What are the key points that differentiate a technical CV from those for other jobs?

CAREER PROFILE

A Career Profile may be more appropriate for technical personnel than a Personal Profile. The experience that brings competence and expertise is of more value and relevance than personal qualities in many technical jobs.

KEY QUALIFICATIONS

For many technical positions, your qualifications and training are the most important things you have to offer. However, if you simply move your Education and Training section to the front page, you risk being mistaken for a collage-leaver without a Career History. The solution is to summarise your education and training in a Key Qualifications section on the first page.

Qualifications and training relevant to the job you are applying for take priority. For example, you may be able to use several computer languages, but only the one or two used in *this* job need to go in the summary. The rest can be included in the Education and Training section.

KEY SKILLS

As well as your Key Qualifications, it's a good idea to include a non-academic Key Skills section outlining your practical and/or managerial skills and experience.

CAREER HISTORY

Concentrate on the areas of responsibility you have covered, the skills you've used and the experience gained.

The examples on the following pages show an outline CV which includes both a Key Skills and a Key Qualifications section, and CVs which make use of some or all of these points:

1. **Outline CV**
2. **James Barossa** – System controller
3. **Larraine Watt** – Psychology research assistant
4. **Alison McInnery** – Computer professional
5. **Robert Murray** – Research Fellow
6. **John Crabb** – Food technician.

(**Your Name** in large, bold type)
(Your full address)

_____

_____

_____
(Postcode)

(Telephone number, including area code)

Career Profile

(A brief, business-like description of yourself)
(Skills)
(Background and experience)
(Career aims)

Key Skills

* (The main skills you have developed)
* (Particularly those appropriate to the job you are applying for)
* _____
* _____
* _____

Key Qualifications

* (The main qualifications you have)
* (Particularly those appropriate to the job you are applying for)
* (Include membership of professional bodies where relevant)
* _____

Career History

(**Name of Company**, usually starting with the most recent)
(Dates you worked there)
(Job title)
(Brief description of what you did)

(Brief description of what you achieved in this position)
* _____
* _____
* _____

(**Name of Company**)
(Dates you worked there)
(Job title)
(Brief description of what you did)

(Brief description of what you achieved in this position)
* _____
* _____
* _____

(Name of Company)

(Dates you worked there)

(Job title)

(Brief description of what you did. Jobs you did some years ago require less detail than your more recent ones)

Education and Training

(Starting with the highest, most recent OR most relevant qualification)
(Name of school, college, or university)

(Dates you attended)

(The qualification you achieved)

(Include brief details of what was covered in the course)

-
-
-
-
-

(Name of school, college, or university)

(Dates you attended)

(The qualification you achieved)

(Name of school, college, or university)

(Dates you attended)

(The qualification you achieved)

(Don't go back further than your senior or secondary school)

(Professional Training)

(Details of training undertaken relevant to the work you do)

- (Qualification or skill achieved)
-
-
-
-

Personal Details

(Date of birth)

(Driving licence)

(Married or single – only if relevant)

(Nationality – only if relevant)

(Interests and activities. Brief details)

(References – usually 'available on request')

JAMES BAROSSA
85 St Luke's Place
Collington
Berkshire
BK6 2JZ

Tel: 0000 0000000

Career Profile

A proficient and versatile System Controller with office-based experience of being a system user, and a clear understanding of both the perceived and actual role of computerisation in office life. Skilful at evaluating problems and communicating possible solutions, and capable of making a significant contribution to the efficiency of any organisation

Key Qualifications

- City & Guilds Diploma in Computer Applications
  — PC Operating Systems – DOS and Windows
  — Unix
  — Work for Windows
  — Word for Windows
  — Excel 5.0
  — Access 2.0
  — Novell Netware

Key Skills

- Supporting, facilitating and encouraging both effective usage and good practice in the computerised office
- Working in close cooperation with users and programmers to clarify areas for change and development
- Liaising between computer personnel and staff

Career Summary

Perry and Wybrowe Insurance Ltd
1985 to Present
System Controller
Supported 200 staff on six sites throughout the South of England using computerised systems:

- Provided help desk for software and hardware queries
- Used VMS and RSX Operating Systems to recover lost data files
- Analysed system performance, identified problems and established probable origin before taking appropriate action
- Logged errors for both software and hardware, and referred on to either programmers or engineer as appropriate

- Installed and implemented communications equipment using X21, Kilostream and Mercury links
- Backed-up data records and transfered to off-site storage
- Maintained hardware and data wiring
- Promoted from Claims Supervisor to System Controller after completing City & Guilds training in 1990, in time to oversee computerisation of organisation

Ambassadors Assurance
1982 to 1985
Assistant Claims Supervisor
Clerk

Education and Training

Central Berkshire CAT
- 1990 – City & Guilds Diploma in Computer Applications

The Willis School
'O' levels: five including Maths and English

Personal Details

Date of birth:	2 January 1964
Health:	Non-smoker
Licence:	Full, clean, UK driver's licence
Interests:	Collecting early silent film and cine film
	Member of the English Film Archive
References:	Available on request

Larraine Watt

Flat 3
14 Deans Gate Road
Waterly
Hertfordshire
HE14 3GN

Tel. 0000 0000000

Career Profile

A patient, perceptive and thorough research assistant, with a specific interest in education and development, especially as applied to adult learning, and practical experience of eliciting, collecting and analysing psychological data.

Key Qualifications

- MSc The Psychology of Learning
- BSc Psychology
  — Advanced statistical analysis
  — Quantitative techniques in applied research
  — Experimental psychology
  — The psychology of education and development

Key Skills

- Coordinating, planning and running experiments
- Collecting data using observation, interviews and questionnaires
- Communicating tactfully and effectively with subjects
- Analysing data
- Writing detailed, comprehensive research reports
- Presenting results clearly and intelligibly

Career History

North London College
Centre for Educational Research
1995–Present
Research Assistant
Conducted research into effects of relaxation and/or stress in learning situations with adult learners:

- Planned and arranged experiments with aim of providing specific research data
- Took subjects through experimental procedures
- Collected and collated results
- Analysed preliminary data by computer
- Prepared preliminary report on findings

University of East England
1990–1995
Research Assistant
Completed BSc and continued to MSc as research assistant to Professor Henry Jenkins, investigating the role of colour in children's play and development.
Assisted as demonstrator for undergraduate zoology practicals.

Education and Training

University of East England
MSc The Psychology of Learning
BSc Psychology (2.1)

Kings Mordent School
'O' levels: eight including Maths, English and Biology
'A' levels: Biology, Chemistry and Sociology

Personal Details

Date of birth: 14 May 1970

Interests: Singing with local musical society
                     Modern and classical music
                     Yoga

Health: Non-smoker

Licence: Full, clean, UK driving licence

References: Available on request

Alison McInnery
91 Southways Road
East Studley
Surrey SR14 4OC

Tel. 0000 0000000
Fax. 0000 0000000

Career Profile
An experienced computer professional with a background in software development for structural engineering research and systems management, now specifically interested in the area of water resources or environmental science, and keen to gain experience leading to membership of the Charted Institute of Water and Environmental Management.

Key Skills and Qualifications

- MSc Water Environment
- BSc (Hons) Ocean Science
- Mapping environmental, specifically hydrological, information via ARC/INFO Geographical Information System
- Using ORACLE/SQL*Plus database technology
- Pro*Fortran programming and environmental modelling

Career History
NAAC
Institute of Hydrology, Pardham 1994–1995
MSc Placement
Mapped river flow data for 1976 drought in Western Europe for completion of MSc dissertation:

- Contributed to UNESCO regional hydrology research project
- Identified gaps in time-series data, providing a basis for future research
- Produced map sequences for Western Europe, aiding presentation of the progress of the drought

Northern Power and Electric
Halford Technology Centre, Nordham, 1986–1991
Second Engineer
Analyst programmer:

- Developed 3-D computer graphics for finite element structural analysis resulting in external sales in the UK and overseas as well as internal use
- Provided CAD system management and technical support for internal and external clients

East Midlands Power Generating Board
Research Division, Stourling, 1980–1986
Technical Officer
Analyst programmer:

- Developed 3-D CAD graphics on IBM mainframe system
- Analysed data from computerised test rig
- Gave technical support on graphics hardware for engineering research throughout UK on network
- Promoted from laboratory technician in 1983

General Employment
1975–1980
- Computer operator
- Mechanical Engineer
- ONC mechanical engineering apprentice

Education and Training
1994–1995 Downland University
MSc Water Environment
- Environmental Information Systems
- Water industry public relations and marketing
- Environmental law
- Project planning
- Operations and finance
- Ecological and adaptive management

1992–1993 University of the South West
BSc (Hons) Ocean Science
- Environmental modelling
- Sedimentation
- Underwater science
- Marine law and resources
- Physical oceanography

1987–1992 Open University
BA Science and Technology
- Computer-aided design
- Geology
- Imaging systems
- Information technology
- Oceanography

Computer skills:
- DEC/VAX and SuperProject system management
- ARC/INFO geographical information system
- Silicon Graphics GL, GraPHIGS and IBM GDDM computer graphics
- UNIX operating system
- FORTRAN and 'C' programming
- Wordperfect, Lotus 1-2-3 and Excel applications

Personal Details
Date of birth:	5 June 1958
Licence:	Full, clean UK driving licence
Interests:	Cross-country running, gliding, swimming, sailing
References:	Available on request

ROBERT MURRAY
12 Henshaw Place
Upper Tithing
Northamptonshire
NP12 3GV

Tel. 0000 0000000

Personal Profile
A realistic, reliable and open-minded researcher with mathematical, statistical and organisational skills and broad experience in social research. A good team worker with a healthy sense of humour who works well under pressure.

Key Skills
- Delivering all stages of a research project
  — Writing proposals
  — Questionnaire design
  — Interviewing
  — Data analysis
  — Report writing and presentation
- Supervising junior staff
- Working with interviewees requiring patience and diplomacy
- Computer literate – Statistical Package for Social Sciences

Key Qualification
- BA (Hons) Applied Social Studies
- Diploma of the Market Research Society
- Use of Statistics in Medical Sociology
- Quantitative Techniques in Social Research

Career History
Northern and Western Medical School
Centre for Research on Drugs and Health Behaviour
1990–Present
Research Fellow
Research Assistant
Conducted research into high-risk (HIV) behaviour of illicit drug users:
- Prepared and designed research project
- Supervised staff
- Interviewed high-risk groups
- Analysed resulting data
- Presented results

The results of this research project and subsequent publication and presentation at conference:

- Validated the use of needle exchange schemes
- Helped attract further funding via other research programmes
- Promoted extension of the scheme with a subsequent increase in staff levels

Rollandson Bookmakers
Tribune Bookmakers
1980–1985 Full-time
1985–1989 Part-time
Manager
Responsible for all aspects of running a betting shop:

- Cash control
- Security
- Managing staff
- Accounts reconciliation
- Dealing appropriately with customers and clients

Education and Training
1985–1989 Polytechnic of the City (now City University)
BA (Hons) Applied Social Studies 2:1

- Sociology
- Research methodology
- Computing
- Social policy
- Statistics

1973–1980 Oxhill Grammar School and College of Further Education
'O' levels: seven including Maths and English
'A' levels: English, French, History

Work-related training:

- Use of Statistics in Medical Sociology:
	applying statistical tests to quantitative data
- Quantitative Techniques in Social Research:
	the application of quantitative techniques

Personal Details
Date of birth: 7 November 1962
Licence: Full, clean, UK driving licence
Interests: Most sports, including football, tennis, golf and snooker
References: Available on request

John Crabb

1 Ascot Lane
Hills Barton
Cheshire
CX14 8JN

Tel. 0000 0000000

Career Profile

A food technician and supervisor with significant experience gained in all departments of food manufacturing from Quality Control to New Product Development, together with a sound understanding of the benefits of Total Quality Management.

Key Skills and Qualifications

- BTEC HND Food Technology
- Extensive knowledge of the food manufacturing industry
- Managing and supervising staff
- Planning and executing product trials to budget
- Implementing laboratory requirements and techniques
- Understanding the importance of marketability and profitability

---

Professional Experience

1993 to Present

Cantrip Farms (Production) Ltd
Barton Magna
Department Supervisor

Worked in supervisory role in all areas of yoghurt manufacturing from raw material to production through to cold store distribution

- Improved process within natural set department
- Reduced wastage in custard-style yoghurt department
- Improved efficiency overall, reducing costs and improving profit margins

1991 to 1993	Hilldean Dairies Ltd

Pollend
New Product Development Technician

Developed marketing ideas into manufacturable products

- Developed key product ranges, improving market placement
- Increased product diversity and, consequently, viability within group
- Consistently brought processing trials in to time and on budget

1987 to 1991 **Farm Fresh Foods Ltd**
Millingham
Senior Laboratory Assistant

Responsible for quality control of all incoming raw materials and supervision of staff in the absence of the Quality Control Supervisor

Promoted from Laboratory Assistant in 1989

Education and Training

1984 to 1987 **Southlands University**
Sunderford
BTEC HND Food Technology

1982 to 1984 **Pentland College of Agriculture and Horticulture**
Pentland
BTEC OND Food Technology

1977 to 1982 **Bower Park School**
Alston
Total of five 'O' levels gained, including Maths and English

Personal Date of birth: 10 May 1966
Driving licence: Full, clean, UK licence
Health: Non-smoker

Interests I have a keen interest in sport and keeping fit and play regularly for a local Sunday football team.

References Available on request

14

CVs for Management Jobs

Managers ensure that things happen as and when they should within an organisation. It's a manager's job to see that his or her personnel can carry out their own jobs effectively and efficiently.

It's essential a prospective employer believes that you will be an effective manager. It's important, therefore, to emphasise your past achievements in your CV, as these will be a good indication of your future abilities.

The key qualities employers usually look for in applicants for management jobs are:

- The ability to get results
- The ability to motivate and manage others
- Competence, reliability and responsibility
- Tenacity and perseverance, along with energy, commitment and enthusiasm
- The ability to tackle problems effectively.

What will help get these qualities across?

PERSONAL PROFILE

Personal qualities often count in management positions. Include a Personal Profile to highlight your special characteristics. Outline your own personal style of management and the experience you've had to develop and exercise these qualities.

KEY ACHIEVEMENTS

Companies want managers who can make a difference to performance – achievements matter. Include a Key Achievements section, either with or instead of a Key Skills section. Let them know what you're capable of doing.

CAREER HISTORY

Put facts and figures to the claims you have made. Rather than just stating your responsibilities, give details of your performance with past companies and expand on your achievements and results.

Your experience of encountering and solving problems is important as well.

The examples on the following pages show an outline CV including a Key Achievement section, and CVs which make use of some or all of the above points:

1. **Outline CV**
2. **Aldwin Hills** – Financial manager
3. **Linda Vernon** – Catering manager
4. **Mark Renato** – Operations manager
5. **Ellen Ashe** – Personnel manager
6. **Lee Daniels** – Technical manager

(Your Name in large, bold type)
(Your full address)

(Postcode)

(Telephone number, including area code)

Personal Profile

(A brief, business-like description of yourself)

(Personal qualities)

(Experience)

(Management skills and strengths)

Key Achievements

* (The main things you have achieved)
* (Particularly those appropriate to the job you are applying for)
*
*
*

Career History

(Name of Company, usually starting with the most recent)

(Dates you worked there)

(Job title)

(Brief description of what you did)

(Brief description of what you achieved in this position)
*
*
*

(Name of Company)

(Dates you worked there)

(Job title)

(Brief description of what you did)

(Brief description of what you achieved in this position)
*
*
*

(Name of Company)

(Dates you worked there)

(Job title)

(Brief description of what you did. Jobs you did some years ago require less detail than your more recent ones)

Education and Training

(Professional Training)

(Details of any professional training undertaken at work)

- (Qualification or skill achieved)
-
-
-

(Membership of Professional Bodies)

(or institutes)

(Name of school, college, or university) (Starting with the highest, most recent OR most relevant qualification)

(Dates you attended)

(The qualification you achieved)

(Name of school, college, or university)

(Dates you attended)

(The qualification you achieved)

(Name of school, college, or university)

(Dates you attended)

(The qualification you achieved)

(Don't go back further than your senior or secondary school)

Personal Details

(Date of birth)

(Driving licence)

(Married or single – only if relevant)

(Nationality – only if relevant)

(Interests and activities. Brief details)

(References – usually 'available on request')

Aldwin Hills
7 White Hart Villas
Wood Heath
Norfolk
NF11 6DM

Tel. 0000 0000000

Personal Profile:
An astute, knowledgeable and experienced manager with a solid background in financial management and a talent for business planning and forecasting developed through working in both manufacturing and services, along with the proven ability to deliver results on time and within budget.

Key Achievements:
- Delivering comprehensive financial planning and guidance:
  - Analysing financial data and monitoring financial control
  - Producing budgets, cash-flow forecasts, and profit and loss projections
  - Analysing and processing productivity records
  - Assisting businesses to develop in a realistic and viable way
- Successfully expanding manufacturing and wholesale business five-fold in seven years
- Improving performance of client organisations by 5–25% overall, including:
  - ABC UK Ltd
  - Xpress Haulage
  - Cornwallis Systems Ltd
- Establishing a venture capital company in the UK on behalf of the parent company
- Bringing the project in on budget and generating £4 million of business in the first three months

Career History:
1995–Ongoing
Management Consultant
Analysed and advised on aspects of businesses finance:
- Advised companies wanting to raise finance
- Compiled guidelines and yardsticks for companies wishing to monitor their performance and develop further, including:
  — Market segmentation
  — Financial controls
  — Production
  — Product/service development
- Prepared and presented business plans, including:
  — Budgets
  — Cash-flow forecasts
  — Profit and loss account projections
  — Break-even analysis

Maynard Investment Corporation (Portland International)
1993–1995
Project Manager
Established UK subsidiary for overseas investment corporation:
- Researched and analysed market
- Created venture capital company and established company's presence in the UK

- Installed and implemented all administrative systems
- Administered all documentation, agreements and financial analyses
- Achieved early break-even by keeping well within budget
- Generated over £4 million of business within three months of UK launch

Preston and Fielding
1991–1993
Financial Advisor
Analysed clients' current situations and future goals. Advised and assisted them to plan and monitor their financial situation. Trained and qualified by LAUTRO.

Hoopers Ltd
1987–1991
Sales and Marketing Executive
Sold, marketed and promoted garden products to single and multiple garden centres and similar outlets.

Willings and Cathar Wholesale Blinds Ltd
1962–1987
Sales Director
Started as general assistant and reached director level with responsibility for group.

Work Related Training:
Computer skills:
CLAIT
List Manager – Xerox Corporation course on building and maintaining databases
Microsoft Works 3.0
Microsoft Office:
    Word 6.0
    Excel 5.0
    Powerpoint 4.0

Other:
Business Planning and Good Business Practice
Taxation, Annual Accounts and the Inland Revenue
Advertising and Promotion
Marketing – Planning and Implementation
Direct Marketing
Negotiating Skills
Customer Care

Personal Details:
Date of birth: 16 September 1945

Interests: Member of the Wood Heath Photographic Society and the Enterprise Business Club, active in the PDSA and the North Norfolk Performing Arts Committee. Enjoys swimming and walking

Car owner/driver with full, clean, UK licence

References available on request

LINDA VERNON
33 Shortmead Road
Allerton
Derbyshire
DB3 5TF

Tel. 0000 0000000

Personal Profile

Energetic, professional and self-motivated, a confident and creative manager with significant experience in both catering and management gained with major employers in the field, and proven skills in setting and achieving goals through the development and motivation of staff.

Key Skills and Achievements

- Six years' experience in restaurant and catering management
- Improving efficiency of service in two significantly different environments
- Successfully introducing comprehensive staff training programmes
- Establishing systems and procedures for a large-scale catering operation
- Managing a first-class restaurant

Career History

La Noisette Restaurant
Lambourne, Derbyshire
1993 to Present
Assistant Manager
Responsible for day-to-day running of restaurant and management of ten restaurant-area and bar staff.
Duties included:
- budgeting
- stock control
- ordering
- bookings
- customer service

Introduced comprehensive staff training schedules resulting in a greatly improved service to customers and the continued enhancement of La Noisette's first-class reputation.

Lambourne Health Trust
Lambourne, Derbyshire
1990 to 1993
Catering Supply Manager
Full responsibility for planning and delivery of catering service to two hospitals, four nursing homes, and four residential facilities.
Duties included:
- full budget planning
- service administration
- management of up to 20 staff

Improvement of service efficiency resulted in reduction of service costs by 12%.

Hollander Catering
Ellerby, Hertfordshire
1988 to 1990
Assistant Manager
Responsible for day-to-day organisation of a commercial catering company including both office and staff administration.
Planned and delivered presentations for company which won two major new contracts.

Cornfleet Country Club
Cornfleet, Sussex
1986 to 1988
Food Store and Cellar Manager/ Banqueting Assistant
Responsible for supervision of all stock ordering and deliveries for cellars and food stores, and organisation of table layouts for all function rooms.

Various
1984 to 1986
Waitress/Catering Assistant
General waitress duties including providing breakfast, lunch and dinner to 550 people daily, and silver service in a five-star country hotel.

Education and Training

Professional Training
Restaurant and Catering Training Association
NVQ level 3 Catering
NVQ level 3 Catering Management
NVQ level 4 Business Management

Dorning College of Technology
Combe, Dorset
1982 to 1984
City & Guilds Catering Certificate

Bordingham Comprehensive
Bordingham, Dorset
1977 to 1982
Total of seven 'O' levels, including Maths and English

Personal Details

Date of birth:	12 April 1966
Licence:	Full, clean, UK driving licence
	Hygiene Certificates held
	St. John's Ambulance First Aid certificate held
Interests:	Active member of local environmental group
	Member of the Wine Society
References:	Available on request

Mark Renato
43 Redding Pit Road
Heath Place
Sussex SX15 8DD

Tel. 0000 0000000

Personal Profile:

An Operations Manager with a total of 15 years' manufacturing experience including seven years at senior management level. An effective communicator and motivator with a track record of achievement in implementing change successfully and efficiently, based on a thorough understanding of engineering processes.

Key Achievements:

- Increasing financial performance of group by £250K overall
- Reducing duplicated operating costs by £100K per annum
- Managing and coordinating activities at three factory sites and ensuring efficient supply of products to customers
- Reorganising and establishing Administrative Support Centre
- Drawing up and implementing change programme in two subsidiary factories, bringing them level with rest of group
- Improving industrial relations, restoring management leadership with help of Partnership Agreement

Career History:

Bishop & Challenger Ltd
Knotting, Sussex
1992 to Present
Operations Manager
Responsible for factories and staff within the operational area.

- Coordinated and managed activities within three factories and an Administrative Centre
- Organised efficient running of sites
- Ensured delivery of products to internal and external customers
- Managed quality control, budget and timetable requirements
- Prepared budgets and allocated capital expenditure

Deans Valley Forgeway Ltd
Mandover, Essex
1989 to 1992
Factory Manager
Responsible for all aspects of factory management.

- Achieved budget production levels
- Administered Health and Safety legislation

- Prepared budgets
- Allocated capital expenditure
- Liaised with customers, notably MOD and Crown Suppliers

Esbarten Engineering Ltd
Stoke, Essex
1985 to 1989
Industrial Engineer
Responsible for engineering services at factory and regional level. Provided production engineering service with particular emphasis on product costing, pre-production engineering and methods assessment and improvement.

Peckham & Been Associates Ltd.
South London
1981–1985
Design and Development Engineer
Designed and developed prototypes from inception through to production.
Promoted from apprentice level in 1982.

Work Related Training:

Computer skills:
CLAIT
Computer Smartware II
Microsoft Office:
    Word 6.0
    Excel 5.0
    Powerpoint 4.0

Other:
    Open University – The Effective Manager
    City & Guilds – Certificate in Mechanical Engineering
    Supplementary Certificates in:
    — Toolroom Practices
    — Inspection and Quality Assurance
    — Health and Safety Legislation
    — Negotiating Skills

Personal Details:

    Date of birth: 1 October 1966
    Interests: Swimming, golf
            Member of East Sussex Choral Society
            Voluntary trainer with the Southey Youth Association

    Car owner/driver with full, clean, UK licence

    References available on request

ELLEN ASHE
91 Stuart Close
Reach
Gloucester GL4 7XS
Tel. home: 0000 000000
work: 0000 000000

PERSONAL PROFILE

An experienced personnel manager with expertise in both human resources and industrial relations, and with general management skills including administration and project leadership as well as overall staff management. An effective motivator and trouble-shooter with well-developed communication and interpersonal skills and a commitment to excellence in human resource management.

KEY ACHIEVEMENTS

- Developing comprehensive human resource policy, reducing staff turnover and increasing efficiency and productivity
- Negotiating Partnership Agreement between management and unions
- Achieving 85% staff compliance with 24-hour telephone banking service
- Introducing Quality Programme of personnel-led productivity initiatives
- Devising and delivering focused induction training course to 350 employees
- Fellow of the Institute of Personnel and Development
- Qualified in the use of psychometric testing and profiling tools

CAREER HISTORY

Cotswolds Financial Services Group
1993 to Present
Employee Relations Manager
Managed overall personnel function for office and general staff
- Undertook:
  — Complete IR function
  — Specialist employment consultancy
  — Project management
  — Social club management
- Developed personnel policies and procedures for financial group
- Improved effectiveness of human resource development strategies
- Managed introduction of performance evaluation system
- Extended skills in all aspects of personnel management
- Developed comprehensive knowledge of employment law, performance management and discipline handling

1984 to 1993
Personnel Manager (Sales Staff)
Personnel Manager (Head Office Staff)
Organised complete personnel function for Head Office and Southern Region Staff
- Managed personnel function for field-based staff, locally-based office and general staff
- Administered records, pay and contractual documents
- Promoted from assistant personnel officer in 1986

1980 to 1984
Personnel Administration Supervisor
Responsible for administration of:
- records
- information
- pay
- contractual documents

1976 to 1980
Personnel Assistant
- Administrative and semi-technical support

Various
1970 to 1976
Clerical Assistant and Officer
- Personnel administration including recruitment, salaries, expenses, cash accounting
- Routine tax returns and administrative duties

EDUCATION AND TRAINING

Work-related training:
- Psychometric testing
- Assessment skills
- Management training courses

Fardean College
1974 to 1976
- 'A' levels: British Government, Economics

Episcopal Secondary School
1964 to 1970
'O' levels:
- Six including Accounts, Economics and English

PROFESSIONAL

Fellow of the Institute of Personnel and Development

PERSONAL

Date of birth:	17 October 1953
Health:	Non-smoker
Licence:	Full, clean, UK driver's licence
Interests:	Table tennis, including running local club
	Photography, City & Guilds qualified
	Swimming
	Music
	Voluntary work
References:	Available on request

LEE DANIELS
42 Cartwright Crescent
St George
Bedford BD12 7GM

Tel.
Home: 0000 0000000
Work: 0000 0000000

Career Objective

A challenging senior management position sought with a progressive company where professional experience and expert knowledge can be exploited to the full. A high level of commitment and professionalism offered in return for challenge, job satisfaction and the opportunity to build on existing experience.

Key Strengths

- Professional management skills
  - Meeting objectives
  - Identifying problems
  - Promoting solutions
  - Managing change
  - Setting and monitoring policy
  - Motivating and developing staff
- Extensive experience of aero-engine overhaul and repair management
- Knowledge of business systems with contracts experience
- Well-developed and effective communication skills

Career History

Eastern Aero-Engines plc

1992–Present

Engine Overhaul Manager

Responsible for developing a sustainable and profitable Sea-horse repair business on engines, components and associated services:

- Achieved planned margins and cash flow
- Developed market opportunities and expanded business
- Negotiated contracts
- Interfaced with customers
- Allocated and managed resources to fulfil target commitments

Also administered closure of East London Repair Facility and transfer to Dublin.

1985–1992

Repair Control Manager

Responsible for administration during contractual changes from Cost Plus to Fixed Price:

- Introduced new working practices to suit commercial environment
- Supervised contract administration
- Coordinated technical control and facility planning
- Maintained customer interface

Engines worked: Sea-horse, SD222 and Blair conversions.

1983–1985
Production Control Manager
Responsible for scheduling and logistic support of engine/module build programmes. Developed mechanical scheduling/monitoring and reporting system.

1979–1983
Inventory Manager
Responsible for order administration and inventory management for new engine projects. Planned and commissioned new Finished Parts Store (£1m project).

1972–1979
Systems Designer
Responsible for SDA system. Trialed SDA packages. Designed order entry systems.

1970–1972
Project Manager
Responsible for bringing B77 engine from development into production.

1967–1970
Section Leader

Qualifications
MIEE
HND Production Engineering
'A' levels: Maths, Physics
'O' levels: Nine including Maths and English

Work-related training:
    Financial Management
    Appraisal Techniques
    Quality Control

Personal Details
Date of birth: 1 June 1945

Licence: Full, clean, UK driving licence

Interests: Sailing
                  Hill-walking

References: Available on request